THE FIFTEEN MOST ASKED
QUESTIONS
ABOUT
ADOPTION

THE FIFTEEN MOST ASKED
QUESTIONS
ABOUT
ADOPTION

Laura L. Valenti

HERALD PRESS
Scottdale, Pennsylvania
Kitchener, Ontario
1985

Library of Congress Cataloging in Publication Data

Valenti, Laura L., 1951-
  The 15 most asked questions about adoption.

  Bibliography: p.
  1. Adoption—United States—Addresses, essays,
lectures.   I. Title.   II. Title: Fifteen most asked
questions about adoption.
HV875.55.V35   1985   362.7'34'0973   84-27936
ISBN 0-8361-3386-2 (pbk.)

THE FIFTEEN MOST ASKED QUESTIONS
ABOUT ADOPTION
Copyright © 1985 by Herald Press, Scottdale, Pa. 15683
    Published simultaneously in Canada by Herald Press,
    Kitchener, Ont. N2G 4M5. All rights reserved.
Library of Congress Catalog Card Number: 84-27936
International Standard Book Number: 0-8361-3386-2
Printed in the United States of America
Design by Alice B. Shetler

90 89 88 87 86 10 9 8 7 6 5 4 3 2 1

This book is dedicated to
adoptive parents everywhere,
but especially to adoptive fathers
like my husband, Warren,
whose silent, stalwart support
is so very much appreciated
and so rarely acknowledged;
and to the work of the Father of us all,
by whose hand these little ones find
their way home to new and loving families.

Contents

Foreword

I happily recommend *The Fifteen Most Asked Questions About Adoption* to anyone interested in learning of a joyous way to enlarge a family. Laura Valenti has carefully collected and recorded the answers to these questions, recounting specific experiences of people whose lives support her statements.

This book is a welcome new resource because the laws and concepts on adoption have changed in recent years. To my knowledge, no other book covers so many aspects of the current adoption scene so well. Until now, prospective adoptive parents have needed to read many books to learn what this one reveals concisely.

In her positive and practical way, Mrs. Valenti answers clearly the many questions asked by people interested in adoption. She explains in detail about children awaiting families and describes the necessity for legislation to protect homeless children. I am impressed with her wise and affirmative view of the needs of older children, of minority and handicapped children, and of sibling groups.

I heartily approve of her emphasis on the love, concern, and time a parent will be able to devote to a child, and on one's desire to adopt, rather than the amount of one's paycheck. Mrs. Valenti knows that the best evaluation of an adoptive family is whether or not they can stretch both their hearts and their budgets farther to include someone new in their family.

Her thorough research on adopting children to handicapped parents is refreshing. One adoptive couple I know are both in wheelchairs and their children are excellently cared for.

The book includes many good tips: (1) keeping a copy of the paperwork involved, (2) being careful, when emotionally strained parents-to-be buy a home, to research wisely to protect both purse and hearts, (3) being persistent in securing professional help for the necessary legal procedures, and (4) taking doubting grandparents to a meeting of adoptive parents and children to share their enthusiasm.

Valenti deals fairly with why people want to adopt children from other races. Individual examples of such adoptees make the experience come alive. The book outlines in detail the specific steps necessary for several types of adoption and warns where to use caution about naturalization of foreign children.

The chapter on adoption support groups explains how the members educate, comfort, and advise people who contemplate adoption or who wait for a child to arrive. I agree with Mrs. Valenti that their newsletters give excellent information.

The cost of adoption is well covered and special needs funds and subsidies are carefully explained.

The author presents in proper balance the challenges,

joys, and benefits associated with adoption. The book gives good advice on how to tell children that they were adopted and why. Mrs. Valenti shares a useful list of organizations that can help in many ways.

The book is easily read, informative, and interesting. *The Fifteen Most Asked Questions About Adoption* shows step-by-step how God can continue to work miracles and change lives through adoption.

—Bertha Holt, President
Holt International Children's
Services, Inc.

Author's preface

*I*n 1979, I boarded an airplane *alone* for the first time in my life. I was headed for Central America, specifically El Salvador (certainly not for the first time), to bring home a new baby son. My daughter and my husband waited anxiously at home. Ten days later, I returned with a sleepy ten-month-old who increased our family to a foursome and started us on an odyssey that has led to this book.

Between the diaper changes of one child, the napping schedules of two, and congratulatory messages from friends, neighbors, and relatives, a message that was thinly disguised in comments, questions, and other assorted bits of information, began to form a complete picture. "Isn't he cute! Can I get one, too?" "Why didn't you adopt an American baby?" "Are you sure you know what you are doing? What you are getting yourself involved in?" "My sister who lives out of state would just love to be able to adopt, too! Can you tell me how you did it so I can tell her?" The whole picture— people woefully ignorant of the regulations and procedures

11

necessary to adopt a child, whether from this country or abroad.

Because we had lived overseas, we knew the children were there. Because we had never hesitated to ask questions (you learn to do that as a writer) or took "no" for an answer (you learn to do that as a government employee if you want to get anything done), we picked up pieces of information about the type of child we wanted to adopt and how to go about it. It never occurred to me that this information was not all compiled somewhere in a neat efficient package. (It was not until later that I realized how lucky we had been to find cooperative sources, and that we had not stumbled into a tangled web of lies—as has happened to other prospective adoptive parents on occasion.)

As more people began to ask me how to adopt, I began to look for a simple single source to which to refer them. But like those just beginning their journey into the serpentine red tape that often surrounds adoption, I was appalled to discover there was no such thing as a single source. The state agency would recite their policies (which might be quite different one county away), a group of one sort or another might know something about international or foreign adoption, but they in turn knew little about local private agencies in the state. Many of the books on adoption were outdated, even those that had been written only a few years before. Others dealt with only a single aspect of adoption. Did we really need to read several volumes to get an overall view? What a hodgepodge mixed-up system!

And so, a few friends and I set to work. For five years we have written letters, collected information, have written still more letters, and have made phone calls to attempt to verify what we learned. We have learned a great deal but still not nearly enough.

We have learned how quickly the requirements for adoption change, which is why no adoption agencies are listed in this book. Few institutions on earth experience more rapid shifts in policies, staff, or procedures than the average adoption agency. The agencies themselves are not necessarily to blame, since they may be working with several government offices, usually are limited to a shoestring budget, and operate in an emotionally charged environment. Prospective adoptive parents encounter enough frustration and misinformation without trying to contact agencies that are no longer in business or those who do not place children outside a certain radius. Local adoption groups usually are reliable sources of information about who is doing what sort of adoption in which area.

We personally have accomplished a great deal, including direct aid and comfort to the families of more than 30 children, newly adopted into a rural area that only experienced its first international adoption in 1979. We still have a long way to go. I have written various articles, booklets, and newspaper stories on adoption. Parts of all of those have been woven into the fiber of this book, which has grown out of the combined efforts of many individuals to reach out to waiting children and waiting families and try to bring them together.

In a few instances I have compared adoption to the birth of a child. I hope this will not be misunderstood. Obviously the majority of the world's children are born into families. In general, people are more familiar with pregnancy and birth and the attending problems than with the adoption process. But adoption is an equally beautiful way to build a family. Some couples who are looking into adoption for the first time are literally on the rebound from a fertility specialist's office who has just informed them they will not be able to produce a child together. I have included these comparisons to give such persons a familiar point of reference. Adoption and birth are both Celebrations of Life and Love and neither can be successfully accomplished in a home that does not have plenty of both.

This book could not have become a reality without the assistance and hard work of many other individuals. I express my sincere gratitude to the following:

To all of the families whose stories have been told here. While their names have been changed to protect their privacy, these are real children, men, and women. They have been open, honest, and candid in sharing parts of their personal lives, thoughts, feelings, and conversations in the hope that they could help others by doing so.

To Linda Splan, a longtime friend and social worker, and a number of her colleagues for reviewing, editing, and greatly improving many parts of this manuscript and encouraging me to complete the book.

To Sister Agnes Irene, Vicki Cravens, and colleagues, librarians at the Kinderhook Regional library, for their research assistance and hard work in locating resource materials and their supportive attitude toward this project.

To Margaret McCorkendale of Family & Children's Services of Kansas City for the loan of the account of Bertha and Harry Holt's venture into Korean adoption, *The Seed from the East* and to Holt's Children's Services of Oregon for permitting me to reproduce a portion of it here.

To Gail Baska of Immigration and Naturalization Services for her help with this book and for many years with many families in the Kansas City region who have adopted children from overseas.

To Bill and Julie Danek for their material and emotional support at every step along the way.

To Laurie Flynn, formerly of NACAC, and Connie Anderson of OURS Magazine, who have taken their time to review specific portions of this book.

To Russ Vogel and family for their encouragement.

To all of those who have so generously lent me their words, both verbal and written, including Carol Sorich of Lafayette, Louisiana, and formerly of the Child Saving Institute of Omaha, Nebraska; Claudia Jewett, one of the most respected authorities in America on the adoption of children; Erma Bombeck, keen observer of modern domestic life and of the American family; Roy Wilkins, respected civil rights spokesman and moral leader; Lori Kellogg of Universal Aid for Children in Miami and Merrily Ripley of Adoption Advocates International of the state of Washington; Glenna Wooderson and Joanne Fulton, both formerly of the Region VII Adoption Resource Center of Columbia, Missouri; Rosemary Taylor of Australia, who is currently working in Thailand; Pam Hoehn of World Children's Fund, now a respected children's advocate and the adoptive mother of a houseful of children, whom I still think of as a friend from high school; and Elizabeth Scott of the American Adoption Congress.

To the North American Council on Adoptable Children (NACAC), Concerned Persons for Adoption of New York & New Jersey, OURS of Minneapolis, World Children's Fund, Missouri Foster Care & Adoption Association, and all the other organizations that keep a steady flow of up-to-date information pouring into our household.

To Pat Adams of World Children's Fund and Eli Butterfield of Butterfield Youth Services for sharing their stories with me.

To Hewitt Associates and Closer Look for the use of their informational lists.

And last, but far from least, my thanks to my husband, Warren, and my children, Francesca and Ricardo, for their loving encouragement, patience, indulgence, and support as I have compiled this book for prospective parents from the many experiences of adoptive families.

—Laura L. Valenti
Lebanon, Missouri

THE FIFTEEN MOST ASKED
QUESTIONS
ABOUT
ADOPTION

1
Who are the children in need of adoption and why?

Wade, 4, is a happy active, apparently healthy child. Born of a white father and a black mother, he suffers from undiagnosed diabetes. He has lived in foster care in one form or another since he was an infant and was severely neglected in at least one home. He is a special needs American child in search of a permanent home.

Micheal, 17, is a good-looking young man with light brown curls, sensitive green eyes, and a soft voice. He should be nearly ready to launch into the world on his own. But Micheal, growing up in the foster care system as it exists today, has lived in 18 different foster homes. Consequently, the word "roots" carries no meaning for him. How can he build a secure life when no one has shown him stability or permanence at any time in his life? At age 17, he is in desperate need of an adoptive family who will teach him how to spread his wings and make it on his own, and who will continue to serve as a safe harbor for him to return to whenever needed.

Sandy is a beautiful 5-year-old girl with curly blond tresses, bright blue eyes, and a ready smile. One look at her photograph reveals a "dream daughter" for many waiting prospective parents. But Sandy is severely disabled from cerebral palsy. She cannot speak, sit up, or walk. She uses a wheelchair and various straps and harnesses to sit upright and eat. A recently acquired lighted electronic device allows her to communicate with the outside world. Trapped inside the uncooperative little body thrives a spirit who giggles often. Sandy is highly intelligent, but needs a real home of her own with a permanent loving family.

Marty, 12, and his 10-year-old sister, *Marilyn*, are on their way to an institution. They have lived in a series of foster homes and have become "too tough" for anyone else to take them. Marilyn has learning disabilities, and suffered some brain damage when one of her foster parents slammed her head against a wall. She has also been sexually abused. Yet, a close look at both of these children hints at what *might* have been, what *should* have been. They are both good-looking children with dark hair, cream-colored skin, and clear brown eyes. Their eyes, however, also hide many things, including the inner hurts and fears brought on by years in foster care. They have seen and learned many things that children should never be exposed to. They also learned to be tough. Life has taught them that to love is dangerous, hurtful, and not worth the pain that always comes when you lose the ones you care about. Is a state institution the only permanent home they will ever know?

Randy, 4, is a healthy white child with big brown eyes and thick brown hair. He is shy and clings closely to his single foster mother, the only parent he has ever known. His biological mother abandoned him when he was six months old and his biological father, an alcoholic and former prison inmate, has never made an attempt to see the boy. His foster mother would like to adopt him and give Randy a "forever home" legally, as well as on a day-to-day basis. Randy's biological father, however, has now decided to claim him, making Randy a legal risk child while a court battle ensues.

More than half a million children, newborn through age eighteen, are in foster care or temporary homes in the United States. No one knows the exact number. While government agencies can report the precise number of benches in our national parks or compute how many foreign cars were brought into this country last year, no single agency or organization in America knows exactly how many children are in foster care or how many of these need adoptive homes. Estimates range from 100,000 to 250,000 children nationwide in need of adoption. The rest are in temporary care situations from where it is presumed they will be returned home or to a relative's home. Or they are in long-term foster care which (in some cases) best serves a particular child's needs. There are thousands of children like Wade, Micheal, Sandy, Marty, Marilyn, and Randy waiting, hoping, and praying that someone will make room for them in their hearts, their homes, their lives.

The average American child in need of such a home is 10 years old, but many are older. Chances are he or she has spent at least one year in foster care, often longer. Some of the children are mentally, physically, or emotionally handicapped. Over half of these children are black, biracial, Hispanic, or Native American (American Indian), making placement into the average white adoptive home difficult. Many of the children are in sibling groups, brothers and sisters who *need* to stay together.

In years past, these children were labeled "unadoptable" and left to grow up in orphanages, mental homes, or the best they could hope for, a series of temporary foster homes.

In the 1870s, Anne Sullivan-Macy, Helen Keller's famous teacher, grew up as an orphan in a Massachusetts poorhouse. She and her brother were locked up with the elderly, the insane, and the dying. They played with rats, cockroaches, and even the cadavers of other inmates who had died. In the 1950s, at age 21, Tom Butterfield (the late founder of Butterfield Youth Services) became Missouri's youngest foster parent in history when he took a normal 8-year-old boy out of a mental hospital. The child was living there because the state had no other place to house him. Compared to the advancements made in other fields over the past hundred years, America's child care standards have made little progress. Despite the country's rhetoric about youth, education, and the importance of childhood, children with no parents to speak for them have continued to suffer. Things are changing (mostly improving) for children without families, but not fast enough to meet their needs.

Older Children. It is still difficult, and understandably so, for prospective adoptive parents who have been planning and dreaming of adopting an infant to switch their thoughts to the adoption of an older child. Many have done exactly that, however, and are now raising families, instead of simply dreaming about it. Old stereotypical patterns and ideas persist that can discourage many. Many have ideas like "An older child can't ever love us like a child we raise from a baby can," or "We want to start a child out in life and work with a 'clean slate,' not correct someone else's mistakes," or "The habits of an older child who comes to us full of rough language and bad behavior will rub off on the younger kids we already have, turning them bad, too." Such ideas can and do stop many prospective parents from thoroughly investigating the possibilities of adopting an older child.

Research has proven all of the above ideas to be substantially false. More important, the same fears have been laid to rest by people who have adopted older children. These children learn to love adopting parents, especially when they come to know how much they were wanted and are loved. The key is "learning to love." Fear of a past is what is expressed in the "clean slate" idea. Older children already have many life experiences, both good and bad, behind them. As a result, they are already people with personality and character that can be seen, heard, and expressed. As adults, people don't reject persons they meet because they don't have a "clean slate." Nor do people assume because they didn't know such persons as very young children, they couldn't possibly grow to love, respect, or cherish them. Somewhat like adults who meet, fall in love, and make a commitment to each other, older children must learn to love and be loved—to make a binding commitment to their new families. In cases where older children are adopted into homes where there are other children, the newcomer will probably be disruptive upon his arrival. However, in the vast majority of cases, the children already a part of the family help teach the newest member appropriate behavior, rather than the reverse.

In the case of an older child who has been abused, rejected, or abandoned in the past, it takes determination and a great deal of love and patience on the adopting family's part before the results will be seen. But thousands of adoptive parents across the country testify to the fact that it is well worth the effort.

> Red, brown, yellow, black, and white,
> They are precious in his sight;
> Jesus loves the little children
> Of the world.

Minority Children. Black and other minority children make up over 50 percent of the children available for adoption nationwide (a disproportionate number—the 1980 census figures list the total minority population of the U.S. at just under 20 percent of the total population). The reasons for this unequal proportion of minority children in need of homes vary. The overall lower socioeconomic level of many minority groups has placed many children in jeopardy and left them without homes or viable substitute homes. The vast majority of social workers have been (and in many places still are) white. Recruitment of minority homes for these children has been limited or nonexistent. Children have been removed from their homes at times more from a lack of understanding and communication between the minority parent(s) and white social workers than because of a home situation without redeeming qualities.

Adoptions by black families are now a growing national trend but it has been a painstakingly slow process. In the past, blacks did not normally engage in formal adoption proceedings. A black family took in a cousin, other relative, or neighbor child to raise but no formal adoption was undertaken. Nor did they adopt a stranger's child, an unknown child, as many white families did. Today's black adoptive families, like their white counterparts of twenty or even ten years ago, are generally young infertile couples in search of an infant with skin tones that match their own. Tragically, a black teenage boy is currently the child least likely to find an adoptive home.

Meanwhile social and cultural support organizations and various adoption and child welfare agencies, both professional and volunteer, continue to disagree on whether it is best to place black and other minority children with white, sensitively educated families, or continue to wait for minority family recruitment programs to produce results. Several groups have strongly protested the placement of black, biracial, Latin, and Native American children in white homes, claiming that nonethnic families cannot give the children the same emotional and mental support and ethnic identity that life in a family of their own background can.

It must be pointed out that many white families are anxious to raise, love, and nurture these children to the best of their abilities. These same families often seek out informational and emotional support systems in their community to aid their children and their entire family. (Some families who have not been allowed to parent American minority children because of social service agencies who oppose the idea have adopted black children from overseas.)

What will best serve the interests of minority children undoubtedly lies somewhere between these two viewpoints. Clearly, there are not enough black and other minority families and individuals ready to adopt the waiting minority children in need of adoptive homes. More efforts and resources must be directed toward recruiting black, Latin, and Native American families if we are ever to come close to meeting the needs of these children.

In the meantime, to insist that any child continue to shuffle through a series of foster homes, languish in an institution or in any other substitute for a permanent loving home, when a home is available—because of race, color, religion, or foreign language spoken—is ludicrous. Likewise, to move a child from one home to another based solely on ethnic criteria is equally ridiculous, as well as dangerous to the child's well-being.

The Indian Child Welfare Act of 1978, passed by the U.S. Congress, was a bureaucratic attempt to correct and clarify this issue, but it has also greatly complicated the adoption of American Indian children. While the theory behind this legislation was to ensure the cultural well-being of Native American children, it may well contribute to longer stays in foster care for all American Indian children. The law states in part that American Indian children will be placed with American Indian families whenever possible, but like similar policies at state levels directed toward blacks and other minorities, no "reasonable length of time" is ever spelled out regarding how long these children must wait for an appropriate family. In many cases, white social workers discourage adoptive parents from considering the adoption of an Indian child. "It's too complicated. There are too many regulations involved," they tell prospective parents. Others simply refuse to undertake such a case. And the children continue to wait.

Using children's issues as political footballs in power plays by government and agency personnel at all levels is a chronic problem that permeates most types of adoption. The American Indian situation is only one example of this. The players of such games are always adults but the ultimate losers are the children, and it is an area in which all parents and child advocates must be wary.

White families can and do love their minority children, as black and other minority families occasionally have the opportunity to love and raise their white children. This may not fit some stereotypical ideas of how things should be (all the black beans together in one basket, all the white beans in this one, all the red beans here). With proper education, cross-cultural adoption *can* provide homeless children with the love, support, and nurture they so desperately need for healthy growth.

Handicapped Children. Only in the past ten or fifteen

years have American families in search of children for adoption awakened to the fact that physically, mentally, and emotionally handicapped children are not "unadoptable." With education and support groups springing up across the country, individuals, couples, and families are now adopting children in wheelchairs, children with cleft palates, diabetes, epilepsy, Downs Syndrome (once known as mongolism), cerebral palsy, spina bifida (sometimes called open spine), and other types of physical and mental disabilities. Even children with cancer or muscular dystrophy, who are literally dying, are finding families who will love and care for them.

Those who adopt the handicapped are occasionally referred to as sainted or blessed, a label at which these parents immediately rankle. "We're the ones who are blessed by having the opportunity to raise such loving children," says one adoptive mother of several Downs Syndrome children. "They love so beautifully and unconditionally. One who hasn't been around such children cannot really appreciate how loving they are."

An adoptive mother of a young daughter who is severely handicapped by cerebral palsy puts it another way, "To be the parent of a handicapped child is to be needed. My other children are busy with their own projects, school activities, or whatever. But this one depends on me and that is something I need and enjoy."

The decision to parent a challenged child, as handicapped children are often called, may seem difficult at first. But most of us already have at least one family member or friend who was handicapped in some way. We may have a brother who is diabetic, a cousin who has epilepsy, or an uncle, an aunt, or a neighbor who has some crippling disease. Familiarity with a certain type of handicap can make other disabilities much less frightening and foreboding. Fortunately, a couple who finds mental retardation too difficult to deal with, may feel comfortable around children with physical disabilities, and vice versa.

In some cases, depending on the cause and type of handicap involved, the condition of the child may improve after adoption. Security, loving parents, and a permanent home are often the best therapy a child can receive. Sometimes children improve beyond the expectations of their doctors and therapists because now they have a reason to try— someone who truly cares about them. (Some types of handicaps, obviously do not improve significantly even in a loving environment. But with the advocacy of a concerned parent, better care may be provided.)

With the development of adult residential centers in most population centers, handicapped adults now have a choice of living in their parents' homes or having their own apartment at a residential center upon reaching adulthood. These centers offer disabled individuals the opportunity to live independent adult lives while still providing them the shelter and special facilities they may need to make it on their own. (See pages 205-209 for a complete list of national organizations that offer aid to the handicapped.)

Sibling Groups. While it is difficult at times to find a home for one older child, obviously the problems increase when there are two, three, or more children in a group— brothers and sisters who desperately need to stay together. When children have been shifted from one temporary home to another and social workers and other professionals come and go intermittently in their young lives, their only constant contact may be their own siblings.

In her book *Adopting the Older Child,* Claudia Jewett, one of America's foremost authorities on the adoption of older children, writes:

> Children separated from brothers and sisters may never re-
> solve their feelings of loss, even if there are new brothers and
> sisters whom they grow to love. There may be more drive in
> adopted adults to track down their remembered biological sib-
> lings than there is to locate their original parents, so great a
> hole does the loss of a sibling leave in one's personal history.

Adopting more than one child at a time can be a risky
business as more time, care, and specialized attention will be
required by each child. Children who band together against
adult authority in a family can greatly disrupt homelife.
However, most child welfare professionals and nonprofessionals agree, the benefits to the children of placing siblings together far outweigh the disadvantages involved.

Fortunately, ready-made families *do* appeal to many couples. Up to seven children in a single sibling group have
been placed together in one family in the Midwest, once
again proving that no child or children are unadoptable.
Vigorous, imaginative recruiting finds energetic, loving couples and individuals who are willing to supply the special
needs of such children.

The reasons why children need adoptive homes (what
happened to their original parents?) are as numerous and
varied as the children themselves. Each child has his or her
own story. In many cases, there may have been only one
parent in the child's life from the time of birth. If that single
parent became ill—either mentally, physically, or emotionally—he or she may no longer have the capability of caring for the child. In difficult economic times, the incidence
of child abuse, neglect, and abandonment may rise. Hard
times for all often translates into especially hard times for
children. They may be involuntarily removed from their
parents' care at such times by state or local authorities. Occa-

sionally the children are voluntarily relinquished by a parent who can no longer cope.

Most children available for adoption have spent some time in foster care. Many spend years waiting and desperately needing a permanent home. Many children available for adoption need to retain contact with biological relatives—grandparents, half brothers or sisters, foster parents, or others. Such placements, called open adoptions, can pose problems for social workers who must seek adoptive parents who will consent to this continued relationship. Such an arrangement can work wonders for a child who can look forward to a secure future without being forced to slam the door on a loving part of his past.

Usually a child available for adoption has some biological relatives still living, although they may not be in a position to care for the child. The child who is suddenly orphaned when his parents are killed in an auto accident or air crash belongs more often to the world of Hollywood script writers than reality. It often takes a thoughtful, well-educated joint decision by social service agency personnel, the relatives in question, and the adopting parents to determine whether continued contact will serve the child's needs in the best possible way.

Children find themselves in need of new homes for a wide variety of reasons. The urgent question is how we, the adults upon whom these children depend, find suitable adoptive families for them in the quickest most effective manner possible.

2

Where have all the babies gone?

(And why can't I have one?)

*I*n years past, the vast majority of children adopted in the United States were white, healthy newborn babies. Most agencies were kept busy matching hair color and eye color between the baby and his future parents. In many areas so many infants were available that couples could practically order the age, sex, and coloring they wanted in a baby. (At the time, a two-year-old was considered an older child.)

Today the baby boom is over in more ways than one. Almost all of the babies adopted in years past came from unwed teenage mothers. Many times the private adoption agency also ran a home for unwed mothers where a young woman could stay for the last several months before her child was born. She simply "disappeared" for a few months. Few members of her family knew where she had really gone during this period of seclusion. In many cases, they were told she had gone to visit friends or was studying at a distant school. In this way, if a young woman chose to keep her "shameful secret" to herself, she could do so, and many did.

Throughout the 1970s and now in the 80s, several factors have had a major impact on the number of infants relinquished for adoption. Birth control became more widely available and many young women, especially those in their 20s and 30s, chose this option. While many teenage girls experiment with various birth-control methods, some discard them as "too confining and/or inconvenient," while others simply remain ignorant. Still other young girls find birth control devices too difficult to obtain without their parents' knowledge or consent.

Though not legalized until 1973, abortion has always been a way out of an unwanted pregnancy. Previous to the Supreme Court decision, abortion had been an expensive but attainable alternative for the wealthy and upper middle class who could pay for an accommodating doctor's services. For the very young, the poor, and the uneducated, it was dangerous as well as relatively expensive. This latter class of abortions were performed by poorly educated midwives, half-trained medical assistants, and other "backdoor butchers," as they were sometimes called.

Other abortions were self-induced. They often left a girl in danger of life-threatening hemorrhage or infection. She could suffer such severe internal damage as to render her childless for the rest of her life. Fear of prosecution kept her from seeking legitimate professional medical assistance so that such severe complications were not uncommon. Nationwide legislation put an end to this illegal, dangerous trade. The number of abortions, however, has grown significantly. According to figures from the Statistical Abstract of the U.S. 1981 and the U.S. Center for Disease Control, approximately 40 percent of unwanted teen-age pregnancies since 1978 were terminated by abortion.

The most significant factor, however, to affect the

number of newborns available for adoption is a major change in society's attitude toward unwed mothers and their children born out of wedlock. Somewhere in the late 60s and during the 70s, as a side effect of alternative lifestyle experiments, couples living together without marriage, and the feminist movement which helped women realize they could make their own way in the world with or without a man, the shame and stigma that had long been attached to a single unwed mother and her fatherless child began to crumble. Young women began to keep their babies and raise them alone or with the aid of their extended family or close friends.

For the older unwed mother with established employment, this was not such a revolutionary decision in many ways. It definitely changed her personal lifestyle, but single parenthood as a result of divorce has been a growing trend for the past twenty years. In many instances the father contributes substantially to their support.

The dark side of this trend lies with the thirteen- through twenty-year-olds who make this decision. Who raises their babies? The average American teenager is not emotionally prepared at 14 or 16, or even 18, to handle the enormous responsibility of raising a child. But currently, nine out of ten teenage girls who give birth decide to keep their babies. For many, it seems the exciting thing to do. At a time in her young life when she is uncertain if anyone really loves or understands her, including herself, the thought of having her own tiny person who will love her totally and unconditionally is absolutely overwhelming and irresistible. Romantic fantasies of childhood can cloud the realities, especially in the beginning. Peer pressure and parental concerns can make even the discussion of adoption as an option impossible. As one biological mother put it, "You can lie, steal, cheat, or commit murder and people will forgive you and find excuses for you, but if you give away your child, you are the worst person on earth." Of course, this is a myth. But it is a prevalent one, especially among impressionable teens.

Unfortunately, for these young mothers the romance fades quickly in the face of dirty diapers, sleepless nights, and trying to support a growing baby on the meager funds provided by federal and state assistance programs. In some cases, the young girl stays at home where she is still considered a child herself. Her parents, now young grandparents, assist or assume the task and responsibility of raising their grandchild. In less fortunate cases, the youngster struggles alone with her baby.

Although there are no statistics to prove it, many child welfare experts feel a large number of these babies do eventually end up on the adoption market—not as easily adopted infants, but years later when the young mother can no longer cope. She may be forced to choose between a new boyfriend or lifestyle and her child, who by this time has often been neglected and/or abused. Soon he or she will be one more special-needs child in search of an adoptive home. (Statistics prove that the daughter who is the result of an unwanted pregnancy is more likely to become a young unwed mother herself.)

Recent budget cuts in social welfare systems, both public and private, have contributed to this spiraling crisis. At one time, a young woman considering giving up her child for adoption would have received preplacement counseling and equally important, post-relinquishment counseling. She would not have been pressured to give up her baby immediately, whether she wanted to do so or not, but professional counselors would help her feel comfortable with her decision, whatever it was. Post-relinquishment services helped her ease back into a normal life, find employment, and generally feel like a whole person again, for what was gained if one young life had been redeemed by the destruction of another? Those agencies who do a thorough job in this seemingly nonessential area, many of them private agencies, find themselves placing the few infants that do become available for adoption.

As for these babies, they are still few in number. For every white healthy infant who becomes available for adoption, there are 50 couples, whose homestudies are already completed and approved, anxiously waiting. Some arrive at their new homes through private adoption or private agency adoptions (see chapter 12). A very few agencies, such as some of the Catholic organizations, still maintain homes for unwed mothers. Fees are high (adopting parents often pay the medical and counseling expenses of the young mother and the baby), waiting lists are long, and requirements are often strict. In short, the competition is fierce.

Most prospective adoptive parents are best advised to explore other means of adoption. They are much more likely to be among the disappointed couples who continue to wait, than the delighted recipients of a newborn baby.

3

Who can adopt?

(Don't you need to have plenty of money, own your own home, and/or be a saint?)

O tis is a tall powerfully built black man with a touch of gray in his hair, a very intelligent, thoughtful, and soft-spoken individual. His wife, *Anita*, is a diminutive Puerto Rican woman from New York with long straight black hair, a nose that crinkles up when she laughs, and a shy but friendly personality. They live in a racially mixed community where they rent an apartment and both work in a nearby industrial area. They would like to adopt a child.

Elizabeth and Chad live on a Midwestern farm with their two half-grown healthy biological sons. Elizabeth has curly blond hair and a gentle voice which belies her inner strength. Chad has brown hair and green eyes and their two sons look like both of them blended together. Their one great hope as a family is to adopt a daughter.

Sid and Sarah are a middle-aged couple with no children. They have always dreamed of children of their own and have had many foster children in their home. Sid and Sarah are both heavy-set individuals with a rough manner in their speech, but a close look reveals two people who care deeply about each other and about the children in their care. Sid is the wage earner and Sarah is the homemaker. Both are active, enthusiastic church members. Sid has a ready laugh and Sarah's strength is almost hidden behind a quiet smile as she holds a child gently but firmly. They both know the true meaning of the word commitment and are committed to adoption.

Lorraine, a single woman in her late twenties, works in a factory and lives in the lower-income housing district. She has been a single foster mother for several years. While she appears to be a shy, quiet young woman, she fights for the children in her care like a mother grizzly. Lorraine wants to adopt her foster son.

A large number of prospective adoptive parents are surprised to learn that public agencies and many private ones have few rules and criteria for adopting parents that are written in stone. A set annual salary, ownership of a home, compulsory membership or attendance at church are not listed as adoptive parent eligibility requirements. Adoptive parents live in apartments, mobile homes, and rented houses. Agency interests today rest more with the love, concern, and time a parent will be able to devote to a child than the amount printed on his or her paycheck. Most agency financial requirements are similar to the following:

> An applicant for adoption must provide financial information and demonstrate their ability to manage their resources to meet family needs.
> —Missouri Division of Family Services Manual

A farm family who lives largely from their own agricultural products may earn only a few thousand dollars per year and yet provide for a child without undue stress to their finances. An executive whose income runs to nearly six figures could prove to be unacceptable as an adoptive parent if his income is so thoroughly absorbed by investments, new purchases, and the like, that he has little left to meet the needs of an additional family member. Obviously, most adopting parents fall somewhere in between these two extremes but it should be realized that there is no hard, fast answer to the question, "How much money must I earn to be able to adopt?" Of much greater concern is how prospective adoptive parents use the resources at their disposal and whether they can stretch both their hearts and their budgets a bit further to include someone new in their family.

The same holds true for the race, religion, and age of potential adoptive parents. With children of all races and religious backgrounds available for adoption, prospective parents of all races and religions are strongly encouraged to apply for adoption. In the majority of cases, social service agencies prefer to place minority children in families of the same race or nationality. Many times a relinquishing mother's only request is that her child be raised by parents of her own religion. Some private religious agencies will place children only with parents of the same religion. Others, though they bear a religious agency name (such as several of the Catholic agencies), work with prospective parents of all faiths. The only way to determine which does which is to inquire.

Most agencies, both public and private, insist on a minimum age of 21 for adoptive parents. While some private agencies have a maximum age for the adoption of infants, most have no maximum age requirement for the adoption of older and special needs children. Middle-aged persons are encouraged to adopt older children. But if younger adults are experienced with teens, they are often allowed to adopt youngsters older than what they might be expected to have if the children were born into their family.

Agencies who work with foreign children have widely varying requirements, depending upon the country and culture with which they are working. For instance, several agencies working in Asia have a minimum-age requirement of 25 for prospective parents and a few have a minimum age limit of 30 years of age. Oriental culture places a greater emphasis on age as a mark of maturity than Western countries. By the same token, these agencies usually have a higher age limit for those adopting an infant.

Over all, children are being adopted into families where they fit, where people want them for what they are. If the adopting parents are not the stereotypical white, young devoutly Christian or Jewish suburban couple of years past, it does not matter. A large portion of the children in need of adoption do not fit into that particular mold anyway. Many public agencies have developed special parent recruitment programs, as have different parent support groups. The emphasis is to encourage *all* types of families to take a closer look at adoption.

Single parents once totally barred from the adoption process are steadily making gains throughout the United States. Singles are adopting both American and foreign children in growing numbers. In most areas, it is still extremely difficult for a single parent to adopt a healthy white infant or toddler. Competition with waiting couples is simply too fierce and a majority of agencies still feel more secure placing a baby in the traditional two-parent family.

But some agencies are finding the single adoptive parent to be the *parent of choice* for a school-age child. Some children cannot deal successfully with the competition for time and affection that comes with the two-parent experience. These children may feel shut out by two adults and find building a relationship with one new parent to be a much more satisfying experience.

Some foreign placing agencies and a few countries overseas still do not accept single applicants for adoption, but a great many do welcome single prospective adoptive parents. Both single women and men are successfully adopting children of all ages from overseas.

The majority of single adoptive parents are women but men are also adopting. While single men may meet more resistance from agencies who are at times uncertain or inexperienced with single adoptive fathers, fortunately for all singles, the barriers are slowly tumbling down. This is due primarily to hard work and persistence on the part of single adoptive parents themselves.

Similarly, handicapped persons are also being allowed to adopt. Grace Sandness, author of *Brimming Over,* the story of her own life, is the adoptive mother of twelve children. She is paralyzed from the neck down from a bout with polio when she was a young woman. Today she and others continue to work to open many doors for the handicapped, including the one marked "Adoption."

Handicapped individuals have been to court and won their right to become and remain parents despite their disabilities. One such parent, William T. Carney, who was left quadraplegic after a 1976 Jeep accident, took his case all the way to the Supreme Court. Their decision in his favor stated in part,

> the ... court should inquire into the person's actual and potential physical capabilities, learn how he or she has adapted to the disability and manage its problems, consider how other members of the household have adjusted thereto, and take into account the special contribution the person may

make to the family, despite or even because of, the handicap.°

Glenna Wooderson, a social worker with the former Regional Adoption Resource Center system, stated the case for handicapped parents even more clearly when she wrote:

> We as social workers can do more for the handicapped than give them parking spaces, restroom facilities, and access to buildings. We can give them access to a more fulfilling life for those who have the commitment and desire to parent by considering them as a valuable resource for the many children who wait. Many times they have more to offer a handicapped child than a non-handicapped family. Perhaps their home is already modified to accommodate a wheelchair, or they can help a handicapped child deal with this handicap psychologically and emotionally by setting an example and truly being able to empathize with the child. Let's not lose out on these resources for waiting children because we do not understand the handicapped. It's our responsibility to learn about handicaps so we can be fair to adoptive applicants as well as the handicapped children in our caseloads.°°

As for perfection in any parent, adoptive or biological, that is obviously just another myth. Adoptive parents are people and as such they get angry and discouraged, cry, lose their temper, forget things, struggle with their marriages, make mistakes, and have no magic answers, just like all parents. As a California father of nineteen special needs children once put it, "A saint doesn't yell at a kid when he or she needs it. A caring parent does."

As a group, adoptive parents have generally given more thought and study to parenthood than biological parents. In

---

° In re: Marriage of Carney, 24 Cal. 3d 725; 157 Cal. Rptr. 383, 598 P. 2d 36, pp. 725-726.

°° From *Handicapped Parents: Why Not?* by Glenna Wooderson M.S.W. Region VII Adoption Resource Center, Grant # DHHS 90-CO-1985-02, Department of Health and Human Services, School of Social Work Extension Program (reprinted with permission).

today's tough adoption market, one thing is certain—there are no accidents. One cannot unintentionally adopt as can happen through pregnancy. One of the special qualities important in adoptive parents is a deep abiding love for children and plenty of persistence. Adoptive parents need an extra measure of the latter to deal with the bureaucratic tangle that entwines the modern process of adoption.

And, after this long process, the waiting and hoping and praying are over for:

—*Wade and Otis and Anita,* who become a family together, and in a few months, when Wade's diabetes surfaces, he will be one of the lucky ones, a child with a mother and father to love and care for him, through sickness and in health.

—*Sandy,* who will now have two older brothers who will delight her, as so many things of this world delight her. She will grow and go to a public school on a part-time basis. Her new parents, *Elizabeth and Chad,* will fight for her right to attend a school with normal children since she will have to survive in a world of normal people. Elizabeth will be needed and busy, as there is extra work with a handicapped child. But it is work that she enjoys since Sandy is such a buoyant, happy child.

—*Marty and Marilyn* never make it to that institution. *Sid and Sarah* intervene, convincing state agency personnel to give the kids one last try. The road isn't easy. There are many bumps along the way—family counseling and a few great battles—but progress along the way is clearly visible. Marilyn's smile is seen often and Marty now resembles a normal busy 12-year-old boy more than a suspicious fugitive. Both children's eyes begin to reflect something new, something they have never dared trust before, a commitment to stay, to learn, to love and be loved.

—*Randy*, whose foster mother, *Lorraine*, has won her two-year battle in court to keep and adopt her foster son, the son she has raised since he was a tiny infant. Now both mother and son can relax, knowing they are a family who will stay together.

No family comes forward for *Micheal*. He turns 18 and the courts adjudicate him, declaring him to be an adult—at least as far as making his own living arrangements and finding a job are concerned. Payments to his foster family stop and he is forced to leave their home. With no money, no job, no skills, and no idea of where he will go, what he will do, or who he really is, this young man has been turned out on a world and by a world that does not care.

Current statistics show that up to 70 percent of those in prison in the state of New York spent some time in foster care during their childhood. Tragically, this is the tomorrow that awaits far too many teenagers today who are living in foster care, needing to be adopted before, like Micheal, their time runs out.

4

What is a homestudy?

(And why do I need one?)

*L*inda changed her clothes three times that morning before nine o'clock. She couldn't decide whether to wear jeans and a sweater or dress more formally in a dress or skirt and jacket. She fussed with her hair. Her husband Frank's best efforts to remain calm and nonchalant were unconvincing also.

As she walked through their tiny four-room house, Linda swatted at real and imaginary flecks of dust with a cleaning cloth, even though the entire house was all but spotlessly clean. Frank's palms were wet and clammy and he paced and chattered nervously, although he normally presented a quiet, calm exterior, no matter what the situation.

"I wish this house was bigger and in better shape, and that other renters had been kinder to it," Linda complained. "The walls have so many nail holes in them and the wood floors are so scratched and sloped."

"There's nothing we can do about it," Frank assured her. "Don't worry. It will be all right ... really. We aren't going to live here forever, you know." Frank tried hard to sound reassuring.

Contrary to how it may seem, Linda and Frank are not expecting a visit from snobbish relatives, influential business contacts, or even the IRS. None of those can inspire attacks of anxiety that compare with that brought on by the first visit from the adoptive social worker.

Old stereotypes and ugly stories continue to portray the homestudy as a grueling inquisition in which such minor details as the wrong clothes or the condition of the walls of a rented house could seriously jeopardize the final approval rating on a prospective adoptive couple.

In one sense, a homestudy is exactly what its name implies—a study of one's home. In reality, a homestudy is simply a good look at one's home, lifestyle, and medical history by both the social worker and the prospective parents themselves. A homestudy is really a dual education experience.

A good homestudy should help the social worker become better acquainted with the adopting parents so that she can understand what type of child they want and what type of child will best fit into their lifestyle. Some children need more structure and close supervision than others. Children with such needs can be more closely matched with a compatible family when the social worker has an accurate picture of a couple's homelife.

A homestudy is not a white-glove test of a person's housekeeping methods. As one social worker explained, "I have to worry a bit about a home where nothing is ever out of place. It makes me wonder if such a family will be able to deal with a real-life child who will naturally spill or break a few things or leave toys, shoes, and mittens underfoot from time to time."

Another social worker put it this way. "On my first visit to a home I can see and smell that the entire house has been cleaned from top to bottom, but by the third or fourth visit, the prospective parents begin to relax and I will see a few dirty dishes in the sink or an unmade bed as they come to the realization that, just like them, I'm human and not interested in checking the top of the refrigerator for dust. How they feel about children, deal with children, live with children—that's what's important."

The basic homestudy consists of three parts: (1) forms to be completed by the prospective parents, (2) interviews conducted between the social worker and the prospective parents, and (3) a finished homestudy report written by the social worker.

In the first step, facts such as birth dates, marriage dates, personal references, and employment history are listed. These are filed along with certified copies of birth certificates, the marriage license, any divorce decree of a previous marriage, and similar documents. Prospective parents are asked to write down their feelings about various types of children. Many prospective parents have difficulty completing a form which consists of a long list of handicaps and illnesses. They are asked to check whether they could accept a child with a hearing loss, blindness, seizure disorder, mental retardation, and many other possible disabilities.

While the task of completing such forms can be exhausting, it does force prospective parents to think about various handicaps in a new light. Parents should keep in mind that these forms are provided to give the social worker and the parents themselves an idea of which handicaps the parents feel they could or could not accept in a child.

The forms can also be a good starting point for a social worker and prospective parents to discuss their feelings about handicapped, older, biracial, and other special needs children. Waiting parents should remember that what they write on these forms is not a binding promise to accept any particular child, and that whatever they write, their feelings will probably change as they learn more about adoption and children in general.

Some social workers ask adopting parents to write their own autobiographies. This may sound like a difficult task, but producing an impressive work is not the point. Social workers are interested in an adopting parent's childhood. How was he or she raised? What are his thoughts, feelings, and beliefs on parenthood? What does she think her own parents did right or wrong? How would he raise his children differently? What experience have these prospective parents had with children of different age levels? What type of child do they want and why?

Obviously, there are no right or wrong answers. One director of a rural social service agency recalled a handwritten autobiography that filled less than two pages in which a middle-aged farmer who had not completed high school related his desire to adopt a son. Although his autobiography was barely legible, he clearly expressed his love and concern for children and why he felt he would be a good father. His homestudy was approved.

As in all government transactions involving extensive paperwork, prospective adoptive parents should make a copy of their homestudy papers, forms, and certificates before returning them to the adoption agency. This will give them a record of exactly what they wrote for future reference. And if the agency copy of their file is lost, a copy is readily available so that valuable time is not wasted, waiting for a missing file to be located.

All agencies require prospective adoptive parents to complete medical questionnaires, have a thorough physical examination, and/or obtain a statement from their physician regarding their health in general. Few agencies require, as in the past, that prospective adoptive parents *prove* the fertility or infertility of either parent. The majority of those seeking to adopt are still those unable to bear children themselves but this is changing rapidly. Many adopting parents are also biological parents and have both children who are adopted and children who are born into their family.

After the original papers and forms are completed and returned to the agency office, the second step in the home-study process begins. A series of from three to six interviews between the parents and the social worker are conducted in the adopting parents' home and in the adoption agency's offices, when convenient. The worker usually interviews the couple together and then individually so that she can learn more about their individual personal histories and know them as persons rather than as mere collections of data appearing on the various forms.

The social worker will want to discuss the couple's reasons for applying for adoption. If infertility (whether documented by a doctor or not) is a factor, a good social worker will review the matter with prospective parents to be certain they have worked through the pain and disappointment involved and are ready to move past their grief to another phase of their life as a family.

As the social worker learns more about the prospective parents through the interview process, so the parents also learn about themselves and what they want from their family life. For although adoptive parents are sometimes viewed as more altruistic than other parents, like all parents, they want something for themselves as well as to help a homeless child. That something may be love, gratitude, the joys and challenges of child rearing, the completion of their family as a unit, or any number of other emotional gratifications. A skilled social worker can help parents discover what it is they hope to gain from an adoption and also to determine if their particular expectations are realistic. Illusionary or unfulfilled expectations can undermine any family relationship, adoption included.

A state social worker active in adoption and foster care services for over six years reported that in all the homestudies she had done, she had only turned down one couple. "Most people," she said, "can see or feel for themselves when they are not ready to bring a child into their life. They withdraw voluntarily or put the homestudy process on hold until existing problems can be resolved."

Some prospective adoptive parents, like Frank and Linda, worry unnecessarily about details in the homestudy process. Their home was approved after three visits from the social worker. When Linda confided to her worker that she had been concerned about the house and its problems, the social worker smiled. "While this house is not elegant, it is also not so bad as you seem to think. You've done a good job of making it into a comfortable home. With your husband moving up in his career, you won't be here long. But more important, you and your husband have an enthusiasm for life. And your history shows you have experience with working with children of several age-groups. That is much more significant than an uneven floor or a few cracks in the plaster."

Prospective parents are also concerned with how much they should tell the worker concerning their past life. Obviously, it would be unwise not to report such items as a past marriage and divorce or anything else that is a matter of public record. More intimate details—such as an adopting parent having been raised in a child-abuse situation, or an adoptive mother who years earlier gave up a child for adoption—may not be documented. But such information can be of enormous help to the social worker as she tries to determine which child will best fit into which family. It is important that prospective adoptive parents share anything that may in the present or the future have any sort of effect on the adopted child or the family's life and relationships. Prospective parents can use the homestudy interviews as a time to review major events in their own lives and how they have dealt with them. In any homestudy, an important issue is how individuals work together as a family through difficult as well as good times.

In some cases, prospective adoptive families may find they cannot communicate with the social worker that has been assigned to them. They can and should contact the agency again and request a different caseworker if they feel that a conflict of personalities will affect their ability to share pertinent information with the social worker.

The interview process may stretch over several weeks. While this is frustrating to prospective parents who are in a rush to adopt, there are several reasons for this slow pace. Most social workers carry an extensive caseload. Many must deal with foster care and abused and neglected child concerns as well as adoption cases. Unfortunately, adoption cases rate last in priority on this list.

By allowing time to pass between interviews, neither the adopting parents nor the social worker acts in haste. This is important for both parties. Time to think and consider all aspects of the adoption can only help all concerned. Time has its limits, however. A couple who does not have regularly scheduled interviews, or other contact with the social worker between interviews, should not hesitate to contact her every other week to be certain their homestudy progresses at a normal pace and has not become lost in the bureaucratic shuffle. The old adage "the squeaky wheel gets the grease" applies in adoption proceedings, provided it is not overdone.

Upon completion of the interviews, the social worker submits her final report to the agency office personnel to be typed. While few public adoption agencies actually provide a copy of the homestudy to the adopting parents, prospective adoptive parents do have the right under the Federal Freedom of Information Act (1974) to see and read their homestudy. This can be an important step.

Throughout this chapter, the phrase "a good homestudy" has been used. Unfortunately, not all homestudies fall into this category. A good homestudy *should* give an overall picture of a prospective adoptive family, their home, and their life. The written homestudy is the *only* reference a child-placing agency will have to acquaint them with a prospective family for a child they hope to place. If a couple's homestudy is sent to another city, county, or state, that homestudy needs to present a clear picture of that couple if they hope to adopt a child through that agency. A two-page homestudy that gives no more than basic data on a prospective adoptive couple will not measure up when compared to a warm descriptive ten-page study of a couple which reflects their willingness to adopt special needs children, their parenting skills, and life experiences with children of various ages.

Agencies in many metropolitan areas now offer group homestudies, in which a number of prospective adoptive couples and singles are brought together by the agency to learn about the adoption process as a single group. Instructors often include experienced adoptive and foster parents, in addition to one or more social workers. While a few individual sessions are still conducted to obtain and confirm personal information, much of the learning goes on within the group structure. This provides an enriched experience for all, as the various prospective parents share opinions and perceptions on the adoptive process.

The major reason behind discrepancies in the quality of homestudies is a lack of properly trained social workers. Social workers continue to receive a great deal of poor publicity and many adoptive parents have stories to tell about uncooperative or blatantly hostile workers. However, adoption in the United States is a state responsibility, and not that of the federal government. Training and requirements vary widely from state to state. With one or two exceptions, the amount state treasuries dole out to children's services departments is pathetically inadequate. As in all professions, a few social workers are lazy or uncaring or hampered by their own prejudices. Others find themselves caught in political squeeze plays between higher echelon personnel, but the vast majority are truly interested in their cases. And many are highly dedicated to their work, determined to do the best job possible. Still, far too many adoption case workers have had little or no special training in adoption.

Lack of training may mean little until the consequences are realized. It can show itself in small ways, such as a lack of professionalism. A social worker may seem too cold or too businesslike with prospective adoptive parents—especially since the subject being discussed is children who love and need love and are the lifeblood of any family. Or as discussed earlier, it can be seen in a two-page listing of facts and figures that is loosely called a homestudy and reduces a family's love and desire to raise children to a few pages of computer-like statistics and dates.

Lack of training can also be observed when adoptive applicants are turned down because the social worker does not agree with their political, religious, or social views, did not like their house or their lifestyle, or some other relatively minor aspect of the family's life. The basic question—can they parent a child, giving him or her the love, respect, and support needed to become an independent, self-respecting, loving functioning adult in society?—gets lost in peripheral issues that a biased social worker deems more important than a child's need for a permanent family.

And once a child is placed, an untrained social worker who has failed to provide post-placement services and support can watch a disaster unfold if an adoptin disrupts or fails, because she did not have the skills to help the family through this time of adjustment.

Prospective adoptive parents caught in a situation where homestudy needs are not being met should not feel as if they are being held hostage by the system. Many private adoption agencies will conduct a homestudy for prospective parents. A large percentage of parents adopting foreign children must contact a local private or public agency to do their homestudy as they work with an out-of-state child-placing agency, which cannot conduct a long-distance homestudy.

Private agency charges for the homestudy vary from approximately $500 in the Midwest to nearly $1,000 on the West Coast. Public agencies usually provide a homestudy free of charge, since they are government-supported, but several state agencies will not provide homestudy services for those adopting foreign children. Obviously, adopting parents should not have to pay for a private agency homestudy to adopt a state-supported special needs child. However, many things are not as they should be in the various state foster care/adoption systems. Those who want to become adoptive parents should be prepared to fight a system of red tape and bureaucratic tangles in order to turn their dreams into reality.

There is no easy solution to all this red tape or to prospective parents' questions as to *why* it is all necessary. It can be particularly frustrating to an infertile couple who watch others produce children in a seemingly effortless manner or hear of abused and abandoned children that no one wants. Perhaps no one has provided a better answer than one official of a Midwest state children's services agency who said, "Social service agencies are asked [by taxpayers and legislators] to justify their expenses and activities more than any other government agency."

Every effort must be made to be certain that the children in the care of such agencies, literally in the public's care, go to caring, loving, permanent homes. This is not simply the responsibility of social service agencies but of the entire community.

5

What is foreign adoption?

"Fear not for I am with thee. . . . I will bring thy seed from the east, and gather thee from the west; I will say to the north, Give up; and to the south, Keep not back; bring my sons from far, and my daughters from the ends of the earth" (Isaiah 43:5-7). The Word of God is quick and powerful, or as the Revised Version puts it, living and active, and I felt that perhaps God might use me to save even more of His little ones than the eight that we hope to bring back.°

With these words Harry Holt ended the first of many letters he sent home to his family waiting in rural Oregon, as he traveled throughout South Korea in May 1955, less than two years after the Korean War had officially ended.

Harry Holt and his wife, Bertha, were humble farmers who believed in putting their evangelical Christian faith into action. They and their six biological children adopted

___

°Reprinted with permission from *The Seed from the East* by Bertha Holt, Oxford Press, 1956.

eight Amerasian infants and toddlers from war-torn Korea after seeing a missionary's films on the severe discrimination, malnutrition, and neglect these children suffered after being left behind by their United Nations servicemen father.

On his first trip to Korea, Harry Holt spent six months readying paperwork and collecting his new family. In the meantime, he and his family were interviewed by *Time, Look,* and *Life* magazines and seen and heard on various national and local news programs on radio and television, a real jolt for this retiring family. As a result of all this publicity the Holt family found themselves inundated with over 500 letters by the time their new children arrived. These letters came from couples all over the country who also wanted to adopt GI babies, as Amerasian infants were called at that time. Foreign adoption had begun in earnest in modern America.

Harry Holt could not know the prophecy of his words at the time. The 1955 trip to Korea was only the first. A few months later, the Holt Adoption Program began. It became the first major adoption agency to place exclusively foreign children in the United States and later in Europe. Harry Holt died in Korea in April 1964. He is survived by his wife and his many children, both biological and adopted, all of whom continue to support foreign adoption programs and activities.

The Holt family was shocked at the national interest generated by their efforts to reach out in love "to the least of these" as directed by their faith. They were overwhelmed and overjoyed to discover that hundreds of other families also wanted to adopt Korean infants and toddlers, despite the lack of information about the children's health problems, personal histories, or ethnic and racial differences.

This interest has grown and developed during the 30

years that have passed since Harry Holt wrote that first letter home. Evangelical Christians began this mission, but as the years passed, many others have joined their ranks. As social awareness grew through the 1960s and 70s, foreign adoption increased steadily, but slowly. The Vietnam War again brought millions of orphaned and Amerasian children to the public's attention. More Americans began to learn of other homeless, starving, and needy children in many other parts of the world. Others simply felt a need to reach beyond themselves. And, as the shortage of American infants available for adoption became more acute during the last two decades, interest in foreign (or intercountry) adoption exploded.

Foreign adoption agencies also became more numerous. Most early agencies grew out of church missionary programs. Requirements for many were strict. Only couples under age 40 with no previous divorce could apply after being married several years. Infertility tests and results were required. At times parents with biological children were turned away for fear they would discriminate in one way or another against their new children. Many of the first nonchurch agencies were fragile entities dependent on volunteer labor and charitable donations for survival. One agency was nearly destroyed in the early 1970s when its address was printed in a national magazine. The resulting avalanche of letters from couples hoping to adopt, closed the agency for many long months as its staff attempted to respond to the thousands of requests for information. Their frail financial situation was strained to the breaking point. Sadly they had to tell the majority of those who inquired that they were unable to help them directly.

In the 1980s, many of the reasons for adopting foreign-born children remain the same. Those who have served overseas and couples or individuals with the same heritage as the child they hope to adopt often choose foreign adoption. Awareness, religion, desire to help, and the relative ease of adopting younger children from underdeveloped countries as compared to the United States are the major motivations behind this form of adoption.

None of these reasons is by itself complete. Most parents adopting these children would probably find it difficult to categorize the specific reasons behind their own decision to adopt. Not unlike Harry Holt, many find themselves inexplicably drawn to adopt children of a certain race or nationality, even without thoroughly examining domestic adoption first.

Many parents select foreign adoption not as an alternative forced upon them by circumstances, but as their first choice fueled by a desire, a drive, a love of these special children that leads them to adopt children from another culture.

Pam Hoehn, a child advocate for World Children's Fund (a worldwide children's sustenance organization) and the adoptive mother of eight children, from six different countries wrote:

> Face it. There is no logical answer. . . . It is strictly emotional. We *want* (another) child, whether it is our first or our tenth. . . . And we feel we have the love and warmth in our family to accept that child. Maybe some logic plays a part in what age or where from, but even that is basically an emotional decision, probably justified by a little logic. . . . I have concluded that there is really no answer to the question [why], but I now have one that everyone believes: "Because we're crazy!"

The families and the children involved in foreign adoption today cover a broad spectrum as the following true profiles indicate.

Sunny was born in Korea of unknown parents and lived in a well-maintained orphanage until 4 months of age. Then she was escorted to the United States for adoption by *Michael* and *Janet,* a rural Midwestern couple. Michael served in Vietnam and never forgot the pain and neglect he saw there in the children's faces. When he and Janet discovered years later that they could not bear children, Asian adoption seemed a natural alternative.

While Sunny was not a Vietnamese street urchin, she still reflects in a small way this couple's desire to reach beyond themselves and their own country to help others.

Today, Michael is a part-time minister for his church and a full-time industry manager. Janet is an elementary school teacher. Sunny is a beautiful six-year-old with almond eyes and a golden hue to her complexion. Her face is round and framed by long, thick black hair.

A year ago, her life and that of her parents changed again, for the better, when Nicky arrived. He is a Korean-born child and now Sunny's little brother. Although his health was not as good as his sister's, due to abuse in a previous home, he is now making beautiful progress. This family has been built through foreign adoption.

Rodrigo was born in the *barrios* (poverty slums) of a large Central American city. His teenage mother left him at an overcrowded orphanage when he was three months old. Three months later, a volunteer social worker found him to be malnourished, covered with skin rashes from poor sanitation, and suffering from a mouth fungus that made it difficult for him to eat. She took him home where his happy-go-lucky personality blossomed almost as quickly as he gained weight. His pale skin color deepened to its natural tan. (Malnourished children often appear to have lighter skin and hair than they naturally would. The body manufactures less pigment than normal, in order to conserve what little nutrition it is receiving.)

After four months of loving care in this foster home, where he also received excellent medical treatment, Rodrigo's soon-to-be adoptive mother came to take him home to the United States. His new parents, *Lana* and *Wayne*, had lived in Latin America and have a biological daughter who was also born overseas.

Today Rodrigo is a busy kindergartner, growing and developing like any other American youngster. Like all little boys, he enjoys teasing his sister when he gets the chance. The two children have formed a loving brother-and-sister bond. His dark eyes and complexion and jet black hair will continue to bear mute testimony to his Latin-American roots.

His parents, who speak Spanish and English, still have many foreign contacts and encourage both their children to learn about the country in which they were born. This family was completed through foreign adoption.

Tommy was born in Bangladesh and stayed with his biological mother until age 2, when she felt compelled by poverty to relinquish him. He spent several years in an orphanage until age 6, when he was escorted to the United States to be adopted by a large family with 4 other children (two adopted and two of whom were born into the family).

When Tommy arrived in the United States, he was noticeably thin, spoke no English, and was totally unfamiliar with many facets of life that most Americans take for granted. He had already attended school overseas, and he has worked hard to learn English. Barely a year later, he was doing passing work in school. When he arrived at age 6, he became the oldest child in the family, a position he handled well because he was accustomed to helping the younger children in the orphanage.

No one pretends there have not been problems in Tommy's adjustment to this country but he and his new parents, *Gina* and *Larry*, have met these challenges. Gina and Larry had lived overseas before meeting and marrying. They share a deep religious faith and a strong commitment to reach out to waiting children.

Adriana, age 4, is also the adopted daughter of Gina and Larry. She arrived at 7 months of age from India weighing only nine pounds. Extreme malnutrition had severely affected her physically and emotionally. Even at her young age, Adriana was capable of expressing a deep anger and hostility at the poor treatment she had received in her short life. Her parents sought and received help to cope with her many problems.

Today Adriana is still small, wearing size 2 clothes, but a pixie personality and a truly delightful little girl has emerged. Her parents now know the joy of seeing their efforts with this child pay dividends many times over. Adriana has large brown eyes, black straight hair, and a very dark complexion. While her dark skin tone will lead some to see her as a black child, her features are Caucasion.

Her parents are sensitive people who will work to teach all their children to value their original heritage and deal effectively with any discrimination or prejudice they find in the world. As a cross-cultural family, they are fortunate to live in a racially mixed urban community which will offer many resources to the children as they grow. Like many others, this family has found foreign adoption to be a rich and rewarding way to build a family.

Luis was 11 months old and weighed only eleven pounds when his American adoptive mother, *Catherine,* saw him for the first time in a small city in Colombia, South America. She had flown from the United States, her first trip out of the country, to bring her new son home. Her husband, *Frank,* and their 3-year-old biological son waited anxiously on a military base in the states for "Mom" to bring home the new brother.

Little is known about Luis's early life, except that he was abandoned as so many infants are who are born into abject poverty around the world.

Catherine did not walk into this situation blindly. The adoption agency involved had briefed her thoroughly on Luis's health problems. She and Frank had prayed about it and then pushed the paperwork through as quickly as possible, for fear Luis's condition would worsen before they could get him home.

Even so, Catherine was shocked to see a gray-haired, pallid child who appeared to be about 4 months old instead of nearly a year in age. His eyes, however, told a different story. Instead of the "old" eyes or veiled eyes sometimes seen in children who have experienced too much suffering at a very young age, Luis's eyes seemed to snap back at anyone who viewed him with too much pity, "Don't feel sorry for me because I'm going to make it!"

Time, love, and good medical care can work miracles as Catherine and Frank discovered after one year. Luis's palor is gone, replaced by a normal creamy brown Latin complexion. His gray hair has given way to thick black curls, and long black eyelashes grace his brown eyes.

When Luis was nearly 3 years old, he was still not walking, a fact that greatly concerned his American doctors. Catherine and Frank, however, were undaunted. A few months later, they were pleasantly surprised to find their younger son taking his first halting steps.

(It is not surprising that Luis walked later than most children, since he had missed so much of the development which normally occurs during the first year of life. All of his energies were consumed by sheer survival. Although research indicates that severe malnutrition can cause mental retardation and other long-lasting problems, the children listed here who have suffered malnutrition do not at this time show any signs of such problems. These parents do not wish to dispute the findings of scientists, nutritionists, or doctors. But all have traveled their roads to foreign adoption trusting in God, and ready as parents and as individuals to deal with life as it comes.)

Tanya was 3 years old when she arrived in the United States. She has a mellow light brown complexion, dark curly hair, and flashing dark eyes. Tanya comes from the land of the Taj Mahal. Her American parents, *Doris* and *Louis*, have a photograph of her, taken in front of that historic Indian landmark. Doris and Louis were nearing their 50s when they made the decision to adopt. Their biological daughter had died of a catastrophic disease years earlier. While they knew they wanted once again to raise a family, they also knew birth was out of the question and felt the wait for a young American child might be too long.

They had read of the plight of Indian children and had spoken to other adoptive parents of foreign children before making their decision. Theirs was an independent adoption, an adoption undertaken without an agency. A certain amount of risk was involved with no adoption agency to serve as a "safety net" (see chapter 11). But they were prepared to take such a chance. They felt it would shorten their waiting time.

Tanya arrived healthy and exhausted from the 32-hour flight to her new home. She babbled excitedly in her native language to all who would listen and addressed all women as "Momee." Doris remembers several lonely crying spells her daughter went through after her arrival. No one knows exactly what Tanya was saying. But surely frustration with not understanding the abrupt change in her environment and caretakers and her sudden inability to communicate were major contributing causes to her homesickness and to her spells of sadness. Fortunately, these intervals soon passed.

Today Tanya is a beautiful young lady, 4 years old, who has learned English, and goes to morning preschool classes. Her parents are now working to adopt an older Indian sister, a little girl, age 6. They have started a new family life through foreign adoption, where once there were only ashes of a former joy.

The children from overseas, like their American counterparts, cover a wide range. They may be relatively healthy or extremely malnourished. They come from many cultures and their skin tones run the gamut from very dark to relatively light.

Some overseas orphanages are well maintained and properly staffed. However, the majority of such institutions in underdeveloped countries can provide only minimal care at best. Children who are in poor condition when they arrive at such orphanages rarely improve. This is not purposeful neglect in most cases. It is just one more manifestation of poverty-stricken societies in which the majority of the population lives in substandard conditions.

Many foreign children arrive in the United States with what most Americans would consider to be rare or exotic diseases. Malaria, scabies, lice, and various other internal/

external parasites may be unusual in the United States today. But most of these were significant problems in this
country before standardized medical procedures were
adopted in public schools, community clinics, and health
centers. (By comparison, many foreigners would also consider the flu as most Americans know it to be an "exotic"
American disease.)

These health problems (and many others) of arriving
children are usually easily treated through modern medical
techniques, although certain conditions such as hepatitis can
be difficult. Prospective parents are well advised to find a
good pediatrician or family doctor *before* their child arrives,
and discuss with him or her any health concerns related to
the foreign child.

An occasional doctor balks at the concept of foreign adoption or is obviously uncomfortable with the idea of treating
such a child. That is the time for prospective adoptive
parents to begin searching for a new doctor. Most doctors
who have served overseas, treated United States servicemen
returning from overseas duty, and/or who work in a
metropolitan or diversified practice are acquainted with the
problems foreign children might bring with them. Prospective parents should advise their physician in advance,
however, and also discuss how their child's weight, stature,
and general body measurements may differ from the
average American child.

Head circumference, for instance, is a common measurement used by pediatricians to judge normal infant growth.
In a few cases, adopting parents have been needlessly trau-
matized by a doctor who informed them that their child's
head was abnormally small or stunted in growth (suggesting
brain damage or mental retardation) when in fact the doctor
did not take into consideration the child's overall smaller size

or the fact that all persons of the child's particular nationality are of a smaller stature than most Americans.

Furthermore, in many parts of the world children are still raised on heavy doses of superstition and ancient ritual. Many are always laid to sleep on their backs for fear they will suffocate sleeping on their stomachs. Often such children arrive in the United States with a large flat area on the back of their head since soft infant head bones do not harden until a child is 9-12 months old. Some orphanage babies whose beds were against a wall and who were always laid in the crib with their head to the same end, will appear to have a flat side to their head. These flat spots will disappear in a few weeks or months as the baby's head bones harden and round out to their natural normal shape. Such flat spots on an infant's head can also throw off the normal head circumference measurement if a doctor is not aware of this inconsistency.

The head circumference controversy is only one example of the importance of informing a doctor in advance of all known medical information on the child. While most of the children's health problems respond quickly to modern medicine, good nutrition, and regular hygiene, foreign children (like all children) may have more serious problems. Reliable agencies check children as best they can in the home country for serious long-lasting problems, and the United States consulate requires that an approved doctor examine the child before a visa for entrance into the United States, is issued.

Furthermore, as can be seen in the cases of Adriana, Tanya, and even Luis, these children grieve for their homeland and their former caretakers. They are quite capable of expressing anger and outrage at the way they have been shuffled about like so much excess baggage. Each parent must find ways of dealing with the emotional problems inherent to each particular child's situation.

Gina and Larry sought and received professional help with Adriana's problems. Lana and Wayne found both their children, upon arrival in the United States, were nervous at large family gatherings when a great deal of English was being spoken. Lana found if she sat quietly off to one side, speaking Spanish softly near the child's ear, it seemed to have a calming effect. Doris held and comforted Tanya through her spells of homesickness and sadness. At first she found it all a bit frightening. "But when I remembered to treat her as I would have my first daughter in a similar situation and not feel afraid it was the wrong thing, it seemed to soothe her," said Doris.

When one considers the odyssey that these children have passed through to come to their new homes, it is not surprising that they are blessed with incredibly strong spirits, which includes being stubborn at times. They are the survivors. As one adoptive parent put it, referring to another Indian baby, "It takes real grit to pack up bag and baggage and be sent halfway around the world at age 3 months and weighing only 4½ pounds. Why, they won't even release a newborn from the hospital in this country until he weighs more than that!"

Lana put it another way, "Right now, my son and I can have some real tug-o-wars and it is very frustrating at times. But I also celebrate that determination because, someday, when he decides he wants to be a brain surgeon, a professional ball player, or a race car driver, it won't matter how many people say it's too tough. He'll put his mind to it and it will get done, because he is strong enough to make it happen."

As with all children, birth or adopted, foreign children

come with no guarantees, only great stores of untapped potential. Most come from Korea, India, and many of the countries of Central and South America. A few hundred more come from other Asian nations and South Pacific countries. Almost none come from Europe, Australia, or other highly developed nations. The citizens of those countries find themselves in the same situation as Americans and Canadians—without viable numbers of adoptable infants and young children.

The skin tones of the children from other countries and cultures vary widely. An occasional child will be as light-skinned as the average Caucasian American child. But many times, as with Luis and Rodrigo, a child's complexion deepens and darkens with improved nutrition or as the child matures. Many countries have mixed populations in which Caucasian, Hispanic, Negroid, and/or Polynesian racial and cultural traits can be found. All skin tones, facial features, and hair texture types are represented.

Prospective adoptive parents *must* be aware and accepting of this variety and these differences. Foreign adoptive parents who are overly concerned with a child's skin color or race may find themselves on the outside looking in. Most private agencies will not work with parents who want to specify what color child they will or will not accept. Prospective adoptive parents who approach foreign adoption hoping to find a light-skinned child who looks like them should confine their search for an adopted child within their own national boundaries.

Foreign adopted children will never look like their adoptive American parents and this difference must be accepted, even celebrated by the adopting parents. To try to deny it, camouflage it, or ignore it will eventually do serious psychological harm to the child involved. His ethnicity is an integral part of the child and must be welcomed and accepted—just as his ability to excel in music, sports, or mathematics would be—with love and pride.

Children of Far Eastern cultures such as Korea, Vietnam, and Thailand generally share the same Asian traits, such as straight black hair, almond-shaped eyes, and golden and tan skin tone. Amerasian children (children of American or European servicemen and Asian women) have been abandoned by the thousands in the past 30 years as two wars were fought in Korea and Vietnam, and as soldiers and civilian personnel were stationed in neighboring countries such as Thailand. Tragically, Asian society places such a high priority on racial purity that American society's racist problems seem almost nonexistent by comparison. Even young children of Caucasian or black fathers and Asian mothers are tormented, abused, and ostracized by those their own age as well as by older members of society. They are categorically refused a fair education or entrance into any professional career.

Asian society, one of the most ancient on earth, is steeped in tradition and themes of purity and finds the racial melting pot theory which is prevalent in American society to be totally unacceptable for their society. Furthermore, Asians place a high value on one's own family tree. Children who are unclaimed or abandoned by their own fathers are viewed as an embarrassment, something shameful. This does not completely account for the negative attitudes found in Asian society regarding Amerasian children, but it gives some inkling of the rationalization behind this extreme racial purity syndrome.

Some adopting parents find themselves concerned about their child's skin color or racial attributes, not because of their own prejudicial attitudes, but for fear their child will not be accepted in their community. While this is usually not a major problem in large urban areas nor in ethnically mixed communities, it can be a matter of grave concern in smaller, rural, or all-white societies. Adopting parents can and should take positive action to help change negative attitudes.

The director of a well-known adoption agency gave a cryptic answer a few years ago at a national adoption convention to the question "What can we as parents do?" Her one word answer, "Move!" That is one solution, albeit a drastic one. But if that philosophy had been applied in the past, the Irish, Italian, and German (and other nationalities) immigrants to America of years past would have reboarded the ships that brought them here, the first time they were cursed for their inability to speak English like everyone else.

A better answer might be to *think* and *prepare*. Adoptive parents need to be certain of their own attitudes and ready to share them with others. They need to talk with others in their community, obtain their opinions, and share photographs of their prospective child or of children similar to the one they hope to adopt. In this way, they will be in a better position to judge if foreign adoption will be the best choice for the child and their family. Adopting parents will know where they stand and be able to make a well-educated decision based upon their own personal knowledge (see chapter 9).

Such concerns should in all fairness be shared with the adoption agency which will then be able to decide what type of child should be placed in the home. Foreign adopting agencies are interested in the best home for each child. This includes working with the adopting parents to find a child who will grow and prosper in the community as well as in the immediate family.

Foreign adoption agencies have made great gains since the days when national attention would completely swamp their meager resources. Some are still religiously affiliated in one way or another, seeking parents of a particular denomination or general religious faith. Most are small nonprofit organizations which have both paid and volunteer staff members. Most have at least a few employees who are themselves adoptive parents and many have grown from one or two or more families' interest in foreign adoption into a full-fledged child-placing agency. Most are licensed to serve only specific areas such as adoptive parents in one, two, or three neighboring states, and some will work only with residents of a particular city or region.

Foreign adopting agencies' policies differ greatly from agency to agency because they are dependent on so many variables. In the first place, they are totally dependent on the rules and laws of the country of the child's birth. Not only are these rules subject to change at any time with little or no warning but they are, for the most part, incomprehensible to the average American adopting parent. Even when one learns the reason behind the policies and changes (change of government, increased feelings of nationalism, concern that the children are losing their national heritage, change in feelings or attitude toward the United States government, or whatever), it can still be difficult to accept or understand.

Some placement agencies find that certain foreign countries welcome single adopting parents, as well as couples, while others do not. Asian societies place a greater emphasis on age as a mark of maturity, so that some Asian countries will accept older adopting parents and even reject ones they feel are too young (under age 25 or 30). Latin-American countries' age limits on adoptive parents are more likely to be similar to those of most American agencies. Most Central and South American countries still require that one, and sometimes both adopting parents, come to the child's country to take their new son or daughter home, while Asian children are almost always escorted to the United States by another adult. (The adopting parents pay all or part of this person's air fare.) And so the rules differ for each country.

Adoption agency requirements also vary widely from state to state. They are usually licensed and bound by the rules and regulations of their own state and local government. In Ohio, for instance, individual counties determine the legality of foreign adoption, making this type of adoption legal in some Ohio counties and not in others. While most states have specific laws regarding all types of adoption, these laws are often interpreted on a local level, making enforcement and continuity from place to place difficult at best and nonexistent in many cases. Very few federal laws apply categorically to all foreign adoptions with the exception of the rules and regulations of the Immigration and Naturalization Service (INS).

The INS has a specific I-600 form, "Petition to Classify Orphan as an Immediate Relative," which must be completed by anyone applying to adopt a child from overseas. Prospective adoptive parents can receive this form free of charge by calling their local INS office. (The local INS address is listed under "U.S. Government" offices in the telephone directory of any major city. Rural residents can consult their local U.S. Post Office to determine which INS office serves their area.)

Prospective adoptive parents will need to file various certified documents with this completed form when they return it to the INS Office. These documents include birth certificates, marriage license, divorce decrees from any former marriages, and the previous year's income-tax return. Also included with the I-600 form is a set of fingerprint cards for each parent. These cards should be completed in the INS office itself or at the largest most competent law enforcement facility available to assure highest quality. Some parents' completed cards have been rejected in the past because of the poor quality of the fingerprints. The parents were required to make new ones. This takes valuable time, a commodity most prospective adoptive parents do not wish to waste. Once completed and returned to the INS office, these cards are sent to the FBI in Washington D.C. for verification and clearance, a process that takes from six to eight weeks.

The current I-600A form allows parents to *pre-file* their petition for adoption. This means they can file the majority of the needed documents (their *own* documents, as opposed to the child's), *before* a specific child is found. Pre-filing can save adopting parents anxious weeks of unnecessary waiting. If all the parents' documents have been approved beforehand, it takes most INS offices no more than two to three weeks to process the I-600 form and the child's documents (provided they are in good order) and issue a visa clearance to the U.S. consulate in the child's home country. In view of the weeks involved for fingerprint clearance alone, the pre-filing of parents' documents (I-600A) can be a great aid to prospective adoptive parents and their waiting child by dramatically reducing the waiting time involved for document clearance.

While pre-filing is a helpful innovation, it also has its limits. The petition for adoption is valid for only one year from its original filing date. Prospective adoptive parents need to gauge their time carefully so that they can pre-file their documents to allow their fingerprint cards plenty of time for clearance in Washington, and yet not exceed one year from the filing date to the date of the child's arrival.

By now, the entire process may begin to seem an insoluble bureaucratic nightmare of endless regulations, rules, foreign policy, laws, and red tape. In truth, foreign adoption is by its very nature more complicated than American adoption. Adopting parents usually work through a private adoption agency which can help sort out a large number of the tangles. A local adoption support group can usually tell prospective adoptive parents which agencies serve area residents and give them a general idea of what their policies and practices are (see chapter 7).

If parents must rely on their own resources, they should ask any private agency they contact to supply references, especially the names of other parents who have adopted through that same agency. If for confidentiality reasons they seem hesitant to do so, prospective adoptive parents should ask the agency to have a few of their past clients contact them, the adopting parents, directly. If the agency in question refuses to provide reliable references, *or* arrange contacts between prospective adoptive parents and other adoptive parents, then prospective adoptive parents should be wary and consider looking elsewhere.

Because adoption is such a highly charged emotional issue, many prospective parents forget to be cautious and to check things through carefully. They lead with their heart and forget everything else. When one searches for a new house or a new vehicle, when a large financial commitment is involved, prospective buyers shop and search carefully for just the right one. Likewise, although it may offend the sensitivities of some to state it so plainly, prospective parents *must* do their research carefully to protect not only their pocketbooks but also their hearts, before committing themselves to work with any agency.

Prudent planning includes asking for an itemized list of expenses, requesting receipts for all fees that are paid, and asking and receiving straightforward answers to any legitimate questions. While requesting references and receipts may sound like the simple exercise of good business practices, it is amazing and sometimes tragic how many prospective parents do not use common sense when the stakes are so high, and the ultimate reward—children—so valuable.

A reliable agency can outline the step-by-step procedure involved in the adoption of the type of child the parents want. They will know which local, state, and federal laws apply and adoptive parents should not hesitate to ask any questions they have concerning such matters.

By the time they complete a foreign adoption, parents will deal with at least four different governments—local or county, state, federal, and foreign governments. All will play a part in the final placement of the child in the home. Some foreign countries send children to this country as already officially adopted, while other children are classified as being in their new parents' legal custody and must be readopted after their arrival in the United States. (The child-placing agency or the INS office with jurisdiction can tell prospective parents which applies to their child.) Many states recognize adoptions performed in other countries by American citizens while others do not. Adopting parents should check their local/state statutes carefully so that they can determine if their child needs to be readopted through a local court. Any lawyer experienced in family law should be able to help. Many adopting parents readopt in their own state for their own peace of mind, and secure an additional set of adoption papers for their child. In many states, it is a necessary part of the complete adoption procedure.

Adopting parents should also realize that completing the adoption does *not* make their child a United States citizen. Citizenship is a separate process handled entirely by INS and the U.S. District Court system. The local INS office has the needed information on this important final step for bringing a foreign child into full U.S. citizenship here. Parents also need to ascertain that their child will no longer be considered a citizen of their former country. Korea, for instance, must be notified that the child is now a United States citizen. Adopting parents need to nullify the child's Korean citizenship by filing a special INS form, G-641, "Application for Verification of Information from Immigration and Naturalization Records." Citizenship is an issue not to be taken lightly by parents. Children whose papers are not properly filed could run the risk of having no official citizenship.

Despite the intricacies of extra red tape, thousands of American families have been completed through foreign adoption in the past 30 years. It is at times a frustrating process. But as the Holt family and the many others who have followed their lead would readily declare, "It's *more* than worth the effort involved."

6

How long does it take to adopt?

(Why does it take so long and what can we do about it?)

Time

It hangs heavy for the bored,
eludes the busy,
flies by for the young and
runs out for the aged.
TIME.
We crave it.
We curse it.
We kill it.
We abuse it.
Is it a friend?
Or an enemy?
We know very little about it . . .
TIME.

—Erma Bombeck

*T*ime moves slowly for the prospective adoptive parent. One of the first questions most ask is, How long until our child—our very own special heart's delight—arrives? The frustration is not in the question, but rather in the answer, or lack of one. Because no matter how badly a social worker, an agency director, or an adoption volunteer wants to give a direct, concise answer to that question, she cannot. It's impossible because such an answer does not exist.

As we increasingly become more dependent upon precision planning, tightly scheduled routines, and computerized mechanisms, we tend to expect all facets of life to be dictated or arranged in a similar manner. Some, thankfully, are not.

Matching a child available for adoption to waiting parents is still done the old-fashioned way—by human hands, hearts, and minds—not by computer. (While some state agencies are now using computers to give approximate matches, such a computer program turns out 20 or 30 or more prospective matches, so that the actual process of decision-making is still done by people. Usually several individuals are involved.)

When a woman becomes pregnant, she usually has a certain security in the knowledge that at the end of nine months she will know one way or the other that she has a son or a daughter, a healthy child or in an occasional case, a child with certain health problems. She may not always like the final result, but she does have some sort of definitive answer to the question, how long?

The adopting couple has no such timetable. Their work— filling out forms, homestudy interviews, copying family documents begins (instead of taking vitamins, watching the bathroom scale inch upward, and experiencing morning sickness), but they have no real idea of how long it will continue.

Adopting parents are further haunted by ominous rumors and old horror stories that continue to circulate about this or that couple who tried for six years (or eight or ten or twelve) to adopt and finally gave up in frustration and learned to live with (if not truly accept) their lot of being childless. Such a fate need *not* await any prospective adoptive parent, single or married, if they know how to use this waiting time to their best advantage. While no one can say exactly how long a particular adoption will take, prospective adoptive parents must realize that they are the key to their own successful adoption efforts.

The days of prospective parents returning their forms to the agency upon completion of their homestudy, sitting back quietly, and waiting patiently for the social worker to find them a child, are gone, never to return. In today's adoption game, such quiet docile people could find themselves waiting forever. Modern adoption is a very competitive affair. Social workers for both public and private agencies are often overworked and overloaded, processing more cases than they can efficiently handle. This is not usually by choice; it is simply one of the facts of life in the world of adoption. And many social workers have little or no special adoption training to increase their efficiency.

Prospective adoptive parents can quickly find the cards stacked against them unless they take positive action to remove or diminish the barriers that stand between themselves and their goal of adoption.

First, prospective adoptive parents need a thorough adoption education, which may be obtained in a variety of ways. Adoption is *not* a simple subject, and prospective adoptive parents cannot expect to absorb all they need to know in a few hours or even a few days. In some parts of the country, such as the state of Maryland, support organizations offer adoption classes tailored specifically for prospective adoptive parents. In other areas, the public agency or private adoption agencies may offer group homestudy sessions to help future parents learn much of what they need to know about parenting in general and adoption in particular. Many areas of the nation do not have such services available, however, and a great many parents are still quite effectively self-taught.

Prospective parents may begin their search at the public library, reading anything they can find on adoption; foster care; homeless, dependent, neglected, or destitute children; child welfare system(s); foreign adoption/children; adult adoptees; and so on. Persons who think they are interested only in American adoption or infant adoption should still read books on older child adoption, foreign adoption, and adult adoptees. Surprisingly helpful information and also much general information on adoption can be gleaned from a broad variety of books related to adoption and foster care issues. Many public libraries have few current titles on these subjects, but most will request recent books when asked.

Prospective parents should research the latest books and magazine articles, keeping in mind the fast-paced changes that take place in American and foreign adoption. Any information more than a few years old may be out-of-date or even totally obsolete, but even so, the prospective parent may be learning the history of the current state of the child welfare system which is still valuable information for anyone who must work closely with that system.

The public library or the local public service adoption agency should be able to provide prospective parents with a list of private adoption agencies within that state. Future parents should write to each one, requesting information, reading lists, and the rules of that particular agency. (Be certain to include a long self-addressed stamped envelope. Most agencies are still dependent on volunteer labor and operate on a tight budget. Such a courtesy will also encourage a more prompt reply.) Most Immigration and Naturalization Service (INS) offices also maintain a list of adoption agencies approved by INS to perform foreign adoptions and/or homestudies for foreign adoptions. Since some agencies may appear on one list and not on another, prospective adoptive parents will find several different lists helpful. Future parents need to tap as many adoption sources as possible to assure the compilation of *accurate* information, no small task in a field that still abounds with false rumors, myth, and misinformation.

The public adoption agency, the public library, or the community service agency which lists local charitable organizations may be able to provide the names and addresses of the nearest adoption support groups (see chapter 7). Even an organization which is actually a foster parent support group or an adult adoptee organization (often a search group for adults seeking contacts with biological relatives) can help prospective parents find new adoption literature sources. They may know of another adoption group which is more suited to adopting parents' needs.

Prospective adoptive parents need to learn to use the services such groups offer. They may have newsletters, privately owned book collections, addresses of volunteers willing to talk with those interested in adoption, and addresses where more information can be obtained. Prospective parents must remember, however, that such organizations are usually dependent on donations, gifts, and volunteer labor, and not forget to give generously so that they may continue to provide these services to others.

Prospective parents also need to reevaluate their own ideas on adoption. By the time they have acquired a sizable amount of current adoption information, they may feel ready to broaden their own personal requirements on the type of child they wish to adopt. Ideally, prospective parents should learn much of this information during the homestudy period and begin at that time to stretch themselves and their own limitations. Realistically, however, it does not always happen that way. After six months or a year of waiting, prospective adoptive parents should take a hard look at the limits they have placed upon themselves, at the requirements they have set for obtaining an adoptable child.

The couple who is requesting a healthy little girl under age 4 has a much more limited range and will undoubtedly wait much longer than the couple who states they are willing to accept or consider any child under age 12 or 14 and/or a child with certain handicaps.

Agencies, as a rule, are much more willing to work with couples or singles who are willing to consider older children or children with certain disabilities. The agency feels they are more likely to be able to meet this couple's needs and that these prospective parents are flexible, willing to work within the limits of reality, instead of only fantasizing about a perfect, nonexistent child. *Agreeing to consider* a child with certain handicaps is by no means a promise to accept the first child offered by the agency. Many parents refuse to write down that they could accept a child of this or that age or with any specific handicap for fear they thereby commit themselves to adopt only that type of child. Instead, indicating that there is some flexibility on the parents' part, lets the agency know that these parents are willing to meet the agency halfway. Therefore, upon reevaluating their requirements for a child, parents should notify their agency without fail of any changes they feel ready to make. (Most adoptive parents would laugh today if they read again what they wrote on their original homestudy forms. Their perceptions change greatly once they become parents.)

Waiting parents can be assured that they will have the opportunity to read a description and be told about any child offered to them by their agency. They will be able to see one or more photographs and even meet the child (except in most foreign adoption cases) *before* they will be expected by the agency to make any sort of commitment to a particular child.

Parents should not feel that deciding against adopting a particular child will prevent them at a later date from viewing another child. Any reliable agency, public or private, prefers that prospective parents share their hesitancies, their fears, or worries about the waiting child. If they feel certain that this child is not the one for their family, they are expected to say so. A little longer wait, both for the parents and the agency, is certainly preferable to parents who take a child out of fear they will not be offered another. Otherwise, the end result months later could be more hurt, resentment, and a possible adoption disruption.

Finally, prospective adoptive parents should tell *everyone* they know about their desire to adopt. It may come as a surprise but it is estimated that 25 million Americans' lives have been directly affected by adoption. Millions of people know a great deal about adoption and are willing to share that information, provided they know someone is interested and can be helped by their knowledge. So, while it may seem awkward or difficult the first few times, waiting parents need to learn to share their plans with others. After all, a pregnant woman shares her news of expectant motherhood with persons she meets simply by the way she looks. Those waiting to adopt also need to share their expectant news. Many times the benefits will astound all involved.

When Lana and Wayne (see chapter 5) were making their plans to adopt from Central America, they began their search for a child in the conventional way, by contacting an adoption agency upon their return to the United States. This agency regularly placed children from the country in question. But after several months the placement agency notified the couple that because of political unrest they were terminating their operations in that country. Lana and Wayne were devastated. However, instead of giving in to despair, they began contacting old friends who might be able to find a child for them. Most of these contacts were other Americans who still lived overseas. Lana remembered one especially dear friend, a Central American woman whom she did not really think could help, but she felt obliged to ask, if only to avoid any chance of hurting her friend's feelings.

Lana and Wayne never received a reply of any kind concerning the pleas they made to their American friends. Less than four months later, however, their Central American friend called Lana long-distance. They had trouble talking, because the foreign woman was holding Lana and Wayne's soon-to-be adopted son, Rodrigo, a 6-month-old baby boy, in her arms so that he could gurgle and babble across the thousands of miles between them. Lana could only stammer *"muchas, muchas gracias"* through her tears. By telling everyone, even persons they did not really think could help, this young couple saw their dreams of adoption completed.

A note of warning must be injected here. At all times, prospective parents must approach any unsubstantiated adoption offers with extreme caution. If the offer seems "too good to be true," it very well may be and is best avoided. Another advantage of contacting many sources and discussing adoption with many individuals is that waiting parents can better determine if an adoption source is or will be successful, ethical, legitimate, and legal.

As a ball park figure, few waiting parents will see a child in their home in less than 12 months from the time they begin their homestudy interviews, and few families should need to wait more than 2 to 2½ years before a child is placed in their home. To legally finalize the adoption in court will take several more months. All states have a waiting period from three months to up to twelve months from the time the child is placed in the home, or as it is stated in many courts from the time "the parent(s) take legal custody for the purpose of adoption," until the parents return to court for the finalization hearing. At that time the child is pronounced to be the legal child of the adopting couple. This waiting period was designed to give the child and the adopting parents time to adjust to each other before the legal act is made permanent. (It is not designed, as has been mistakenly interpreted at times, to give birth parents an opportunity to reclaim a relinquished child.) Obviously, some adoption cases will take longer than this, especially if unforeseen problems arise. If parents are waiting for a healthy white infant, no one can truly judge how long such an adoption will take or if it will ever occur at all.

Prospective adoptive parents can also cut their waiting time by learning to be persistent and professional. Persistence simply means not taking "no" for an answer. Unfortunately, for many parents and tragically for many children, an appalling number of social workers, agency personnel, and government employees use the word "no" instead of: (a) finding the right answer, (b) taking the time and/or the trouble to do the extra work involved, (c) asking someone else and risk revealing their own ignorance, or (d) all of the above.

To successfully adopt, prospective parents must not simply accept the word "no" and all its variations (that is not possible, that is against our policies, we are not in a position to consider that) without requesting a complete explanation, a copy of the *written* rule, policy, or statute involved, and requesting to communicate with the particular official's superior.

All of the above must be done, however, in the most professional manner possible. Screaming, swearing, or any other rude behavior will only justify the poor performance of the official involved. Persistent prospective parents with a professional attitude who know their facts and their rights are difficult to defeat. The average uncooperative government work (agency personnel, etc.) will often acquiesce in disgust and give the prospective parents what they need, in hopes they will leave and go badger someone else in another office.

Most officials, agency personnel, and others *do* try to perform their jobs well and all should be approached positively. The average person who is approached courteously will respond in a like manner. Prospective parents should *not* confront each new person involved with a combative attitude. Even if they have had problems in the same office before or have heard poor reports about the person involved, parents must give each new individual the benefit of the doubt, believing that they will truly try to help. When it becomes apparent in an occasional encounter, however, that a particular worker is being uncooperative, prospective parents must make it clear that they will stand their ground—not defiantly or belligerently, but with quiet strength and determination.

The same principles can usually be applied efficiently with those who consistently keep prospective adoptive parents waiting for certain documents or forms that they need. At this point, prospective parents must demonstrate patience and wait a *specific* agreed-upon time span. Prospective parents waiting for a homestudy to be typed by office stenographical personnel, for instance, might agree to wait from two to three weeks, once the social worker has finished the study and submitted all materials. Once the allotted time period has elapsed, however, waiting parents should start to contact their agency office once a week to ask if this work has been completed. After a couple more weeks have passed, two or even three contacts per week might be necessary to move the human machinery in question. If an explanation is forthcoming from the office or agency director or other person in charge, prospective parents should again obtain a definite time limit and repeat their tactics until the needed work is completed.

Many worry they will offend the person(s) in charge and then receive no help whatsoever by consistently contacting a particular office or individual. When asking politely, professionally, and persistently for one's own rights, chances are relatively small that any irritation felt by the bureaucrat in charge will adversely affect the results. Prospective parents need to ask themselves, if they are receiving little or no cooperation in the first place, if the risk of loss is truly that great.

One adoptive parent still remembers the vice-consul in a Latin-American country who was unwilling to provide a United States entrance visa for a young teenage student that this parent wished to sponsor. Finally, concerned the teen would disappear and become one more illegal alien, the vice-consul asked the prospective sponsor if she were willing to post a bond.

"Yes!" she answered without hesitation.

"Of $5,000?"

"Yes." The positive reply was the same, although the

woman had no idea where she would get such a large amount.

"Well," mused the vice-consul, "if you'll make the proper arrangements through channels [through the local INS office], I'd only require a bond of . . . say, $500."

Once the sponsor-to-be began clearing the legal hurdles, she again called the vice-consul at his overseas office, outlining the paperwork that would have to come from his office.

Finally, the vice-consul sighed in exasperation, "Stop, stop," he said impatiently. "I will issue a visa to your student and you can forget the bond if you will call her and have her come to my office this afternoon, but only on *one* condition!"

"Which is?"

"That you promise not to call me anymore!"

The visa was issued and the sponsored student came to the United States and studied. The sponsor had an $80 telephone bill that month, but through patient persistence she had won her battle with the particular bureaucratic system involved. (The student never became an illegal alien. After two years of study, she fell in love and married a man in her sponsor's hometown where she still lives today.)

Many adopting parents can do the same. The power lies within their own hands to shorten dramatically the length of time they have to wait to adopt the child they want. They will need to be flexible and willing to work for what they want. It is hard work to constantly pursue the same goal day after day. It is difficult to remain calm in the presence of a government worker who has lost his temper, but whoever said having any child by birth or adoption would be easy? Patience, persistence, and love is what it will take to bring children into a home as well as what it will take to raise them once they arrive.

7

What is an adoption support group?

(And how can they help?)

*I*n New York City and New Jersey, the adoption support groups are called Concerned Persons for Adoption (CPFA); in Minneapolis they have a one-word title, OURS; and in many other places they are called the Open Door Society. In St. Louis and upstate New York they call themselves International Families; in Bakersfield they are the Friends of the World's Children; in Maryland, their name is FACE (Families Adopting Children Everywhere). In Ohio, they are called Project Orphans Abroad; in the hills of southwest Missouri, they are known as Adoptive Parents of the Ozarks (APO). They are all the same and all very different. They are all adoptive parent/family support groups.

The activities of these groups are as different as their names. Many publish monthly or quarterly newsletters. They sponsor fund raising events, help special needs American children find .homes, and send funds and supplies overseas to children who still wait for families in foreign orphanages. Most are nonprofit corporations. On both the state and federal levels their collective voices have been heard as they have written to lawmakers on behalf of the children, both American and foreign, who are without permanent homes and families.

All adoptive parent support organizations have two important functions in common. All exist to provide prospective and adoptive parents in their area with viable up-to-date information on adoption (and in many cases, foster care) issues and concerns. This means they know the agencies, both public and private, that place children in a specific area. They know which ones are reliable, what type of children each agency places, approximately how long the wait will be, and the average fee usually charged. When they do not know, they know how to find out and whom to contact. They also know what printed information is available locally, which public libraries have current adoption books, and which state or local offices or private agencies have pamphlets and other helpful publications available to the public. Many times members share their own books and magazines with each other so that costs and waiting time can be cut dramatically.

Second, the local adoptive parent group provides emotional support to the waiting couple, to the family who has already adopted and is now having some adjustment problems, to the couples or single persons just beginning their quest for adoption information who are totally confused by all the bits and pieces of information—half truth, half myth.

Adoption support organizations provide a unique service in that prospective adoptive parents can attend meetings with other waiting and adoptive parents and see for themselves a 13-year-old American child, recently adopted; a tiny baby, newly arrived from India, Colombia, or Korea; or a 5-year-old who comes from Bangladesh, Costa Rica, or Thailand. They may see a special needs child who has cerebral palsy or Downs syndrome playing with the rest of the children. In this way, they come to know what these children are truly about, instead of depending on their own conjured-up images of what these children might be like. They can visit with others who understand the pain of infertility, the frustration of so much bureaucratic red tape and constant delays, and know that the grief and anguish they feel is real and justified. They can also get a new shot of energy as they see others who have adopted, and learn how to cope with their disappointment and continue the struggle to complete their dreams.

Adoptive family groups also provide support services to the children themselves. It is a comfort to a child to meet others like himself who are adopted, who come to their present families with vivid memories of other places and parent figures, and/or who may not look anything like their adoptive parents.

In many states, especially in large urban areas, parents adopting American children and parents adopting foreign children often form separate organizations. An American adoption support group may actively advocate for other waiting children by encouraging agencies to shorten foster care stays and by working to find homes for special needs children. They may sponsor forums to educate prospective adoptive parents on the needs of these children.

Many organizations maintain adoption exchange books. These large loose-leaf notebooks are usually compiled by individual state children's services agencies, but some are regional and feature children from several states. Each page presents a black and white photograph of a child waiting to be adopted and a detailed description of the child, personality, history, special needs, and conditions. The name of the child's agency, caseworker, or other contact person is also listed. Some agencies that produce these books wish only to be contacted by the agency working with the prospective adoptive parents. Other agencies will discuss these children directly with prospective parents, although most find their social worker can secure more specific information. Other support groups sponsor "match" events. This can be a picnic or holiday party (Christmas, Thanksgiving, Halloween) where several children and several prospective adoptive parents are brought together and visit with each other in hopes that "matches" might be struck between the waiting parents and the waiting children.

Members of a foreign adoptive parent support group usually stand out in a crowd. They find themselves discussing adoption in the supermarket, at the first day of school, and in the doctor's office waiting room. When the child is Korean, Latin American, or Indian, his dark eyes, hair, and complexion (which may run the gamut from very light to very dark) do not match those of his blond blue-eyed parent(s). Those considering foreign adoption for the first time may find this high visibility a distressing or alarming prospect. But parents of a foreign adopted child are used to it. Some even enjoy the extra attention as long as the interest is friendly, because this offers an opportunity to educate others on adoption. Being different has its advantages as well as its disadvantages.

Many foreign adoptive support groups raise funds for overseas orphanages, and sponsor intercultural events, so that their children can learn about their heritage and the land of their birth. Parents are sensitive to issues raised by their children as they grow older and discuss the best answers to comments and questions such as, "Mommy, why aren't my eyes shaped like everyone else's?" "I wish my skin wasn't so dark because the other kids at school call me names." "Why do the other kids always want me to speak a foreign language. I want to speak English the same way they do with no accent." Parents work to help their children appreciate that they are a product of two worlds, two separate cultures. While this can cause problems and frustrations at times, the child needs to respect both cultures and come to terms with this fact. They cannot run away from either, anymore than they can run away from the color of their own skin. Children also learn that their culture is an intrinsic part of them, and a part of why their parents love them.

A few adoptive parent groups in some major metropolitan areas have been formed to support black adoption. These groups work to encourage black couples and singles to take a closer look at adoption, a crucial endeavor since over half of the children waiting across America are minority children. Black prospective parents have tended not to consider formal adoption in the past and have been reluctant to join support groups, but such groups can be of invaluable help to them.

Parents who adopt across racial lines in the United States (Caucasian parents who adopt black or biracial children, or black parents who adopt white or biracial children) may feel as if they are caught between such groups and fit into none. Fortunately, these different groups are not exclusive. Parents adopting American children would usually be welcome in a foreign adoptive parent group or vice versa. But like searching for the "right" doctor or dentist, a family may want to try out more than one adoptive parent support organization before settling on the one that best meets their needs and the needs of their children. Some adoptive parent organizations support all kinds of adoption. These organizations respond to the needs of American adoptive families, families with foreign-born children, and families who adopt transracially.

One last type of adoption support group is established and/or sponsored by a specific public or private agency. This type of group has survived with widely varying success rates. Those begun by employees of the public service agency may not fully serve the needs of prospective adoptive parents because such a group is not free to criticize constructively the agency's performance. Those considering adoption through an agency other than the founding one may be ostracized from the group, and none of the parents would feel free to express their true feelings in such an atmosphere.

Some agency support groups collapse once the organizers move on to other positions or areas. Other units have formed as a result of group homestudy experiments in which an agency, either public or private, has brought a number of prospective adoptive parents together. They work to enrich and expedite the homestudy procedure by imparting general information to the families all at the same time. Such a group may remain an entity only during the homestudy process. But long-lasting friendships may be forged during this time, giving the new families emotional support and joy that endures many years after the study group has been forgotten.

Large private agencies may sponsor support groups, newsletters, and other post-placement support services for families that adopt through their agency. Some of these groups are loosely organized and of little help to the family but others are well-coordinated organizations and offer maximum informational and emotional support to their members.

Almost every state has at least one adoptive support group, and the more populous states have several. Those with newsletters will usually send their publications anywhere in the United States as long as membership fees (or postage and printing costs) are paid. Many of these newsletters are of a high quality, making a member removed by distance feel a part of the organization by means of the printed word.

Collectively, members of adoptive support organizations have written letters and recently influenced major pieces of congressional legislation, including:

- The 1981 tax break giving up to $1,500 in tax deductions on expenses incurred in the adoption of a special needs American child.

- The practical application of Public Law 96-272, The Adoption Assistance and Child Welfare Act, which was designed and passed to prevent unnecessary foster care placements, provide for better case planning by social work staff, provide periodic foster care review, and implement adoption subsidies. (Adoptive families also kept the Reagan administration from combining the funds for this law into his federal block grants [to states] program in 1981.)

- The Amerasian Bill sponsored by Congressman Stewart McKinney and passed in 1982 giving special immigration preference to children born in Korea, Vietnam, Laos, or Thailand after 1950 and fathered by United States Armed Forces personnel or United States citizens working in those Asian countries.

Add to the above numerous private bills which grant special visas to foreign children who for one reason or another cannot qualify for a visa under the normal Immigration and Naturalization Service procedure. (This would include children over age 14 before 1982, and over age 16 after 1982, or children who do not have full documentation, a common problem in underdeveloped countries that are wracked by civil war, earthquakes, hurricanes, and other disasters.) It is obvious that adoptive parents through their support organizations have discovered a combined strength in advocating for children's rights that could never have been achieved individually.

On a local level, adoptive parent groups also make their presence known. They testify before state legislatures on new and updated adoption, foster care, and child welfare laws. They also serve as resources for state, county, and city employees working in the child welfare system. Some agency personnel may not welcome the input of an adoptive parent support organization initially, and others may even feel threatened by the interference of nonprofessionals. Few well-educated truly interested adoption personnel, however, maintain such an attitude if members of the adoptive parent group conduct themselves in a professional, patient manner, demonstrating their concern for child welfare. After all, parents are the 24-hour professionals, living with adoption day and night. (Unfortunately, some agency personnel are not genuinely committed to child welfare. They may feel intimidated and threatened by interested, involved parents, which is their problem, not the parents'.) Experienced social service workers from both public and private agencies recognize adoption as a partnership and usually recommend that new applicants for adoption contact their local adoption support group.

Beyond information and emotional support, adoptive parent organizations can help in a way that is rarely perceived by prospective adoptive parents. Membership in an adoption organization sends a dual message to the child-placing agency approached by prospective parents. It signals that these prospective parents have drive and energy and are not going to wait for agency personnel to hand-feed them every bit of information they need. By making their own contacts and learning all they can without the social worker's assistance, they will save the agency, the social worker, and themselves time and money (especially if it is a private agency charging the parents for the social worker's time). The fact that they are learning basic adoption information through the adoptive parent support organization will allow the social worker to progress more quickly to more specific complicated matters.

Parents will be able to discuss what they have learned with the social worker and secure another opinion on the value of this information. (Sadly, many prospective adoptive parents find themselves educating their social worker on many aspects of adoption. Much of what they have learned may be the most recent information available, and not yet included in a worker's training.) Throughout this entire process, the adopting parents will make a favorable impression on the social worker, which is no small thing when one considers the highly competitive nature of adoption as it exists today.

Equally important, membership in an adoptive parent support group reassures the agency that the child they place for adoption will have a support network available as a continuing resource. This is important to all adopted children, but even more so for children adopted past infancy, foreign children, and transracially placed children. In some rural areas, private agencies will still not consider placement of these special children if such a support system is not available.

There will always be those who feel they do not need such an organization. They may shrug and say, "I'm fine, my kids are fine, and adoption isn't that important in our lives anymore." Sadly, most of the world still views adoption as a second-rate way to build a family, resorted to only by those who cannot have children the "normal or natural" way. Adoptive parent support organizations combat such narrow outlooks and misuses of language and let the world know that adoption is an alternative way to build families through love—neither better nor worse than birth, simply different.

While parents may no longer feel that difference, adopted children progress through various stages of appreciating, understanding, fearing, regretting, and detesting this difference before they can learn to accept it as a significant, yet not overwhelming, part of their life. By spending time with others who share this common experience with them, they find themselves and their families are not so different as they once feared, an all-important discovery for children and adolescents.

Adoptive parent organizations also strive to educate the general public on the use of positive adoption language, using terms such as *birth* or *biological* parent or child, instead of real, natural, or normal to differentiate from adoptive parents or children who have been adopted. It may seem a minor point and yet such seemingly insignificant concerns can add greatly to a child's negative or positive feelings about adoption which will always be a part of his life.

Three national organizations (listed below) maintain directories of adoption support organizations across the country. They will share this information with all persons interested in adoption.

North American Council on Adoptable Children (NACAC)
810 18th Street N.W., Suite 703
Washington, DC 20006
Tel. (202) 466-7570
NACAC is a nonprofit coalition of individuals and organizations working for the fundamental right of each child to grow up in a permanent nurturing home. NACAC works pri-

marily with issues of concern to American special needs children waiting for adoptive homes, and children in foster care placements in the United States. NACAC publishes newsletters, including *Adoptalk*, which reflect the latest news on legislative measuares and policy changes regulating adoption, foster care, and child welfare transactions on federal, state, and local levels. This organization also sponsors National Adoption Week each year during Thanksgiving Week, which is now recognized by an official proclamation of the U.S. Congress. It distributes information packets to adoption support groups, encouraging them to emphasize special needs waiting children's concerns through mass media coverage of special events sponsored by local and national organizations. NACAC also sponsors an annual national conference. Their 1984 convention in Chicago was attended by 1500 adoptive parents and professionals, from the U.S. and Canada.

OURS, Inc.
3307 Hwy. 100 North, Suite 203
Minneapolis, MN 55422
Tel. (612) 535-4829

OURS, Inc. (Organization for a United Response) was founded in 1967 by ten families who had recently adopted foreign children. OURS encourages the adoption of children and child advocacy efforts. Specific efforts are made in material aid to agencies and people in need, manpower aid to local adoption agencies, sponsorship of children overseas, information for prospective adoptive parents and community, recruitment of adoptive parents, cooperation with other groups toward common goals, cultural education, and the promotion of study of adoption and welfare legislation. It publishes a bimonthly magazine, *OURS*, which has a current circulation of 8,000 and is an excellent resource for anyone interested in intercountry (foreign) adoption. There are over 100 OURS chapters nationwide.

NATIONAL ADOPTION EXCHANGE
1218 Chestnut Street
Philadelphia, PA 19107
Tel. (215) 925-0200

The National Adoption Exchange is a national network, bringing children waiting for adoption together with prospective adoptive parents. Special needs children are registered on the exchange by their agencies, and families with approved homestudies are also registered by their agency or they may register themselves. Registration is free. The information is placed in the exchange's computer system and constantly monitored for possible matches. Information on all matches is *simultaneously* sent to both waiting agencies and directly to the prospective parents. While the exchange does not actually place children for adoption, their matching information has proved invaluable in over 400 placements in their first two years. The National Adoption Exchange follows up on all recommended matches, publishes a quarterly newsletter, and is involved in adoptive parent recruitment campaigns with national magazines, radio, and television.

8

How much does it cost to adopt?

*D*epression era mothers used to tell their children, "I wouldn't take a million dollars for any of you kids, but I wouldn't give 2¢ for another one of you, either!" Sometimes, it seems the range on today's adoption costs is almost as wide.

In some Midwestern states, adoptive parents may pay as little as $500 for the adoption of a special needs child, which covers only their basic legal fees. In foreign adoptions, fees totaling up to $6,000 or $8,000 are not unheard of in some Asian adoptions. Legitimate expenses for most adoptions fall somewhere in between.

Because the adoption procedure varies so greatly from one state to the next, it is difficult to pinpoint precise costs. In some states, adopting parents need to pay a lawyer and a private agency each a separate fee. In other states, no lawyer is directly involved, with legal matters handled by the agency itself. In still other areas, even the public service agency (state or county) charges a fee.

To begin, all adopting parents need a homestudy. If the parents are completing the entire adoption through the public service agency, in most states they will pay no fee. The public agency is supported by tax dollars and is designed to serve the public. While this is a fine theory, it does not always work well in practice. A few states (California, for instance) have found their child welfare systems in deep trouble when shrinking tax dollars and exploding populations collide.

Most state/county agencies responsible for adoption procedures must also handle child abuse and neglect cases involving the state's dependent children and also provide foster care. Adoption, to some extent, takes a back seat to these more threatening situations. A public service agency which cannot keep up with its own foster care, child abuse, and neglect cases cannot do a thorough job of meeting adoption needs of the children in their care, and the prospective parents who continue to wait. California has instituted a system of charging parents a fee for adoption services. It operates on a sliding scale, based on the parents' annual income. Still their system, like so many others, is providing inadequate service.

Parents in many states choose to work with a private agency (even though the fees will be much higher). They are not satisfied with the poor quality of service provided by the public agency, which forces parents to wait longer, issues inadequate homestudies which other agencies refuse to accept, and offers little or no continuity because of high employee turnover.

Other state systems, such as that of Minnesota, have risen to the challenge of meeting the needs of their waiting children. Partly spurred by active adoptive parent support organizations and through the considerable efforts of the late

Senator Hubert H. Humphrey, Minnesota probably has the most advanced child welfare system in the United States. Minnesota has pioneered such innovations as adoption exchanges, and their corresponding exchange books, input by parents (adoptive and birth) in forming state policies, and adoption subsidies.

The adoption subsidy now available in many communities is a specific amount of money held for use by (or paid directly to) the adopting parents of a special needs child by the state. Laws and policies on subsidy differ greatly. In Missouri, for example, subsidy is quite adaptable and can be designed for maximum benefit to the adopted child and his new parents.

The subsidy may be drawn up as a maintenance subsidy and paid to the family on a monthly basis for the first few years to help ease the child into the family financially. Use of a maintenance subsidy is quite common in the placement of siblings, a situation in which the addition of several children to a family could become a serious financial burden. As the subsidy period draws to a close, the amount is gradually decreased each month.

Medical subsidy is the most common type of adoption subsidy. It may be designed to cover the cost of any present or future medical condition the child has. It could cover the costs of current medications, or devices such as a wheelchair or leg braces. It may be available until the child reaches age 18, for children like Wade (see chapter 1) who, after placement, was diagnosed as a diabetic. Medical subsidy can help to relieve some of a prospective parent's anxiety regarding the adoption of a child with an unknown medical history. In Missouri, funds for adoption subsidies come from foster care monies. Even if every waiting child in the state were given an adoption subsidy upon placement, the state would still save from $2,000 to $25,000 per child in foster care costs. (The amount depends on the child's age at placement and the actual amount of the subsidy.)

Because the subsidy is paid from foster care funds and administered by the public service agency, no parent adopting a special needs child can be refused subsidy on the basis of the parent's income or with the excuse that the state does not have the funds. The money must be available, for if the child were not being adopted the state would be obliged to continue his foster care payments until age 18. (Subsidy funds were initially controlled in Missouri by the Juvenile Court. However, that system was changed by statute with the support of adoption and foster care support organizations. Few judges actually understood the system and were reluctant to grant the needed subsidies, feeling they were putting the state under a greater financial burden. But actually, adopting children out of the foster care system, subsidy or not, saves the state money.)

Parents have only one opportunity in Missouri to claim subsidy and that is at the adoption finalization court hearing. Otherwise, they lose their chance forever. They cannot make a claim for medical subsidy, for instance, years later if they did not ask for it during the adoption proceedings.

Adoption subsidy exists in varying forms in many other states. Adopting parents may find a number of social workers within the system who still do not understand it well or make regular use of this aid to adopting parents. Adopting parents should make a point of asking a number of state workers and officials about this resource as it applies in their state.

Parents who adopt a healthy white infant through one of the few agencies left in America that still maintain homes or programs for unwed mothers are often shocked at the bills they are expected to pay. Many of these organizations still hold old names, such as "Catholic," "Christian," or "Community Charities," which refer to the days when these organizations took in street urchins, young homeless girls who were pregnant, and other social outcasts. As the director of one such agency once quipped, not without embarrassment, "People want to know how we can continue to use the word 'charities' in our name when we present bills like this?"

Such agencies are actually asking adopting couples to pay the young teenage mother's medical bills as well as those of the new baby. Since teenage pregnancies and deliveries have a higher rate of medical complications, parents may find the bills to be considerably more than they might expect to pay for comparable services for a mature woman. When this amount is added to normal expenses incurred by most adoption agencies, it greatly increases the total charge. The final cost for this type of adoption will often resemble that of a foreign adoption, as much as $5,000 to $8,000.

Parents will also find the competition quite stiff. The requirements will often reflect those of bygone days when no divorces or singles were permitted to adopt and strict age and religious requirements were enforced. These agencies are few and far between and usually do little or no advertising. They are so besieged by those hoping to adopt in a manner reminiscent of 20 years ago—a newborn baby whose origins are cloaked in secrecy—that such agencies are often open to receive applications only a few days every two or three years. The rest of their time is spent selecting homes from the thousands of applicants for the few dozen babies they will have available during the intervening years.

In some states privately arranged adoptions are legal. This type of adoption has in some cases, left prospective parents particularly vulnerable to paying exorbitant fees. While no state has specific guidelines for what a private adoption placement should cost, some states have attempted to control this type of adoption abuse. New Jersey, for instance, has outlawed lawyers and other individuals from acting as go-betweens in private adoption cases. The biological mother is obliged to make the private placement herself in a non-agency adoption. In some other states, to prevent excessive charges, lawyers are required to justify their costs and fees before the judge who oversees the placement. Even with such safeguards, there are lawyers, doctors, and other private individuals working in nearly every state who arrange private adoptions at exorbitant fees of $10,000 and more.

Fortunately, the vast majority of individuals and agencies who work in adoption do so for one reason—to help waiting children and waiting parents find each other, come together, and create new families. A few persons, however, are involved in adoption for what they can get out of it. Prospective adoptive parents must take decisive deliberate steps to protect themselves in all adoption situations, both foreign and domestic.

(1) Prospective parents should *ask for references* from any private agency or individual with whom they are considering transacting adoption business. It may sound hard and cold to refer to adoption as a business but, like it or not, adoption is a business. It is the *good* business of reliable nonprofit private agencies and it is *big* business and *big* money to those few who exploit it for their personal gain. A private agency or individual who works in adoption should be asked to supply specific references, including local well-known and respected business persons in the community.

A prospective parent who suspects there are past or present complaints against an agency or adviser should check with the state's attorney general's office, with the state's office of child welfare, and with the local Better Business Bureau. The prospective adoptive parent should also check with other adoptive parents in their area and with their local adoptive parent support group to find how others have fared with this adoption source. Some adoption magazines and newsletters will publish requests for information from others who have worked with a particular adoption agency or individual.

One single mother paid nearly $10,000 to adopt her 19-month old daughter from El Salvador. The president of a nearby adoptive parent support group was heartsick when she was told, since she had completed a similar adoption for less than a third of that amount.

Prospective adoptive parents should also ask the agency in question to supply the names of others who have previously adopted through their organization. If the agency declines on grounds of confidentiality, waiting parents should ask that some of the agency's former clients contact them directly. If the agency is new, they may not have a long list of former clients but they will have contacts in the field of adoption. New adoption agencies and contacts do not simply fall from the sky. They grow and develop over time and they should know others and be known by others working in adoption. Prospective parents should be extremely wary of any adoption agency or adviser who refuses, no matter how properly and sincerely, to furnish a number of references, former clients, and/or the name of an adoptive parent support group that can lend credibility to the claims made by the agency or individual involved.

(2) Prospective parents should also *ask for a list of itemized expenses* they will be expected to pay. Different types of adoption incur very different sorts of expenses.

Respectable adoption agencies are more than willing to provide their prospective clients with a list of anticipated expenses. In the first place, this allows waiting parents to see they will not, in the case of a foreign adoption, be writing out a check for several thousand dollars. Rather, their expenses will be spread over several months, even over a year or more.

Some expenses like that of the homestudy are fairly standard for a specific geographic area. Other expenses, like that of a prospective parent's plane ticket or hotel bill incurred in traveling to bring a new child home, can be charged to a credit card and paid at a later date. While foreign adoption is not inexpensive, parents can arrange their finances to pay these bills in various ways. Advance planning of expenses and payments is another advantage of having an itemized list.

This is not to say that certain charges cannot or will not change. Most agencies will inform prospective parents of an expected increase. But charges should not suddenly double or increase substantially in an unexplained manner. Such a list of expenses also allows prospective parents to compare likely costs from agency to agency. Although this too may sound harsh or calculating, expectant parents often check out various hospitals, obstetricians, and maternity payment plans. Why should it seem strange for expectant adoptive parents to explore various adoption plans, including the financial obligations they will incur?

(3) Prospective parents should *always obtain receipts* for every payment they make to any adoption agency or any person aiding in an adoption. This may sound simple, but it is amazing how amiable some individuals can be while they adroitly refuse to supply a receipt. One Utah couple paid several thousand dollars to a foreign attorney who was sup-

posed to be arranging an overseas adoption for them. Since they had secured no receipt for their money, they were unable to prove any wrongdoing on his part months later when it became apparent that all the promises he had made to them were little more than empty words. It is difficult to prosecute such individuals and they may continue to operate in a similar fashion for some time.

When prospective parents fear this will be their only chance for building or completing their family, they may grasp at straws, believe almost anything they are told, and pay exorbitant fees without a whimper. Worse, once they realize they have been swindled, they may be too ashamed to speak up. While they nurse their broken hearts in privacy, the guilty party continues on his way, using his tactics on the next desperate prospective parent he finds. The stakes are high, involving that which many value more than life itself—children. Life without children is for many but half a loaf, half a life, a life lived more in gray than in rich full colors.

When prospective adoptive parents keep their emotions in check (no easy task under the circumstances) and research adoption options with the same care they would give to buying a new home or unseen ocean-front property, they will not feel pressured into a dubious or quasi-legal decision. When offered the Brooklyn Bridge for a song, prospective parents who have the facts are prepared to turn and walk away, as well they should.

Prospective parents may find themselves working with more than one agency or adviser in a single adoption. Waiting parents adopting through an out-of-state agency or a foreign agency may need to contact a local agency, public or private, to do the homestudy, since the actual child-placing agency cannot do a long-distance homestudy. The public agency of a state that does not charge for its adoption services may reserve the right to refuse to do such a homestudy, especially if they are already straining to cover their first responsibilities, such as foster care, child abuse, and neglect.

Many public agencies simply do not have the resources, human or financial, to take on more obligations. Some may agree to do foreign or private agency homestudies but only when they can squeeze them in, thereby leaving parents waiting interminably. Other agencies, however, do these homestudies as a public service, believing that the improved public relations generated for the often beleagured public agency by such a courtesy more than pay for any inconvenience in the long run.

Private agencies often do only the homestudy portion of an adoption, but prospective parents who live outside major metropolitan areas may need to search a bit farther than urban residents to find an agency willing to come to their area. Homestudies, whether performed by the actual child-placing agency or by a local agency that is lending a helping hand, are relatively standardized in price for different geographic areas. On the East Coast they cost from $300 to $600, in the Midwest they run from $400 to $650, and on the West Coast homestudy costs approach the $1,000 mark. Once again, other local adoptive parents are the best guide for what a homestudy should cost in any respective area.

Other fees for private agencies placing foreign children vary widely, depending on the individual country where the child resides and the amount of interest the foreign government takes in the adoption of its children to assure quality services; the size, stability, and experience of the agency involved; the quality and amount of service (foster care, medical care, etc.) rendered to the child; and the distance between the foreign nation and the United States destination of the child, which has a great bearing on the price of long-distance telephone charges and airfares.

Again, parents need to check all of the above carefully. Prospective parents may find (as in the case of Korea) that the foreign government is highly involved in the adoption of its younger citizens to other countries around the world and that great pains are taken to assure that conscientious services are provided for the children's welfare. Other countries (like India and those of Latin America) supply many of the foreign children adopted in the United States, but with widely varying degrees of quality in the service provided.

Adoption in India, as in the United States, is a state or regionally controlled matter. While one region may have accommodating rules or laws, another may not. In some Latin-American countries, as well as in some South Pacific nations, government officials and lawyers have sometimes extracted exaggerated fees to further line the pockets of the rich. Unfortunately, many underdeveloped countries have so many other severe problems that they devote few resources to the needs of their abandoned children. This is not to say that parents who adopt from overseas should not seek children from underdeveloped countries or should do so only from nations whose governments have impeccable records. Quite the contrary, these children may need help even more desperately than others, but prospective parents must approach these situations carefully, with their eyes wide open.

On the other hand, when parents see that their child comes from a reputable program or orphanage that is trying its best with the meager resources it has, adopting parents should not forget the little ones who are left behind. No children's shelter in an orphanage or adoption program, foreign or domestic, ever has a full and accommodating budget. There are always unmet needs. Adoptive parents should remember where their child came from and do their best to help in any way they can.

New advances are continually being made to help prospective parents with some of the expenses incurred in American and foreign adoptions. In recent years, a number of private companies have made adoption benefits a part of their general employees' benefits package. Among these companies are:

Abbott Laboratories
American Can Company
Bankers Life
Baxter Travenol
   Laboratories, Inc.
Campbell Soup Company
Control Data Corporation
Digital Equipment
   Corporation
Eli Lilly and Company
Felt Products Manufactur-
   ing Company
Foote, Cone, and Belding
   Communication, Inc.
Gannett Company, Inc.
Hallmark Cards, Inc.
Honeywell Corporation
International Business
   Machines Corporation
S. C. Johnson & Son, Inc.
Lincoln Company
Mennonite Mutual Aid
   Association
Pitney Bowes, Inc.
Proctor & Gamble Company
G. D. Searle and Company
Smith Kline Corporation
Smith Kline and French
   Laboratories
Syntex Corporation
Time, Inc.
Wang Laboratories, Inc.
Xerox Corporation
And the list continues to grow.

A 1980 study by Hewitt Associates of Lincolnshire, Illinois, lists company benefits plans for 14 different companies. These range from a low of $75 paid directly to adopting parents (which was established in 1950 when that same amount was paid for a surgical allowance for pregnant employees) to a high of over $2,000 in reimbursed specific expenses related to the adoption. Most benefits range around the $1,000 mark and are designed to cover agency, court, and legal fees, medical expenses, and foster care and foreign adoption costs.

Increasingly, employers grant the same sort of leave of absence to an adoptive parent that they would to a mother giving birth, and that sums up why companies have instituted these benefits. They point out, as adoption advocates have been doing for years, that it is a matter of equal treatment for all. Many companies feel the relatively small amounts paid in benefits (since the benefit plans are not used often) help improve public relations and generate a corporate image of a company that cares about their employees' personal concerns. (Prospective adoptive parents should check with their employer's personnel or benefits manager or labor union to see if such benefits are available, or if they might be established. The two national adoptive parent support organizations listed in chapter 7 have information on corporation adoption benefit plans.)

On a similar note, prospective parents should check their insurance company's policies regarding medical benefits and other insurance coverage for adopted children. Some companies protect children only once the adoption is finalized. Others cover children once they are living under their new parents' roof. A few even cover foreign children before they arrive in the United States, if the adoption has passed through a foreign court. Prospective parents also need to verify what is covered (such as preexisting conditions) so that they can make plans accordingly.

Other help with expenses is now available to some parents who are eligible as of 1981 for a federal income-tax deduction of up to $1,500 for expenses incurred during the adoption of a special needs American child. Considerable controversy will continue to surround this issue since parents who adopt American children not classified as special needs and the parents of foreign children feel this statute discriminates against them. Several bills that would give deductions to all adoptive parents have been before the United States Congress in the past and will continue to appear until this area of inequality is rectified.

Admittedly, these are small steps compared to the current high costs found in many of today's private agency adoptions, but they are certainly a beginning. The only satisfactory long-term solution will come through people working together to bring costs down. Agency directors, for example, are no more pleased with high fees than prospective parents, maybe even less so. For them it is not a one-time expense to be paid and forgotten, but a fact of life to be grappled with daily.

In the March/April 1983 issue of *OURS* magazine, a bimonthly publication of a national adoption support organization located in Minneapolis, a letter appeared condemning high fees and the inconsiderate attitude of foreign adoption agencies in the placement of foreign special needs children. Lori Kellogg, executive director of Universal Aid for Children, Inc., a Florida-based adoption agency, and Merrily Ripley, executive director of Adoption Advocates International of Port Angeles, Washington, both replied to that letter in the following issue. Their letters, reprinted here, are the best testimony available as to how private agencies themselves view such fees.

Dear Editor:
   As the proud mother of four adopted daughters, two of which are considered special needs and the executive director of an adoption agency, I simply had to reply to the letter in your last column which addressed the following:

   (1) Being upset with amounts private agencies charge for adoptions;

   (2) Questioning study fees which she/he felt should not have exceeded $15 per hour, total $500;

(3) Why an agency could not/would not reduce fees for a special needs child placement;

(4) What can be done about "high fees."

I doubt any person gets more upset with fees that have to be collected than any caring agency staff. Stateside agencies have no control over fees determined by attorneys, liaisons, or agencies in foreign countries. And such fees must be collected at the stage in a case when called for.

Unless a person has long-term experience with case flow from start to finish in an agency office, you are not equipped to determine time spent on a case. While the worker assigned does the visits to determine suitability for adoption placement, there is much work before and after the study. Even with full volunteer staff (except caseworkers) and even with the poorest-looking office, expenses go on. Few agencies are blessed with donated office space, equipment and so forth. Telephone bill, supplies, printing, postage, etc., go on and on.

Adoption agencies are NONPROFIT. They are not [set up] to make money BUT the reality is that funds must be available to continue to provide services.

I have to ponder at this point how little we tend to question the cost of material things we want, such as houses, furniture, automobiles, vacations, designer items, and so forth. Being human, our priorities do tend to get (sometimes) out of order. When we "want" something, we always seem to find a way to satisfy the "want."

Agencies "want" to help children and rarely is a private agency serving foreign-born children fortunate enough to get public or private funding. These specialized agencies have to depend on study fees and private individual or volunteer groups for contributions.

Agencies cannot "reduce fees" for special needs children unless an arrangement can be made with the overseas placement source who has to process the child.

Perhaps the agency the writer mentioned should have been more sensitive to the questions. . . . An effort should be made by the agency to find an "angel" for a very special family and a hard-to-place child they are willing to nurture.

We (UAC) know from beating the bushes, so to speak, that while "angels" are few and far between, they do exist and will help if not abused.

Generally, agencies affix their study fees based on the overall amount needed monthly to operate and provide services; to pay their workers and run the office.

Please keep in mind that while adoption is a human service profession, it is a business. By that I mean certain operating expenses have to be met. Could you imagine a telephone company, for example, donating services? Or even giving you a reduction in your monthly bill?

There is absolutely NO WAY to [establish] uniform fees in foreign lands. Each country has its own laws, rules, regulations, fees, and requirements. . . .

Stateside agencies CANNOT be uniform in fee scale, procedures and policies. Each state has its own regulations. . . .

I have one solution. If every family that ever adopted a child would contribute even so little as ten dollars a month to the agency they adopted their child from, to go into a "Special Kids Fund," then agencies would have funds to help out a family and a waiting child. If adoptive parents got together more and had fund-raising projects to feed such a fund for their agencies, it would be wonderful. What a terrific way to give thanks for the kids you are lucky enough to have to parent.

How many families do you know that once they get their child are rarely heard from again, that ignore plea letters from their agency to help them help kids? Because of their lack of involvement, they "wear out" the dedicated few.

That writer hit on some complex areas of a very sensitive subject. Most of [these] cannot be solved unless agencies and families work together as a constructive unit to solve the problems of the hard-to-place kids.

Lori Kellogg

Dear Editor:

I wish to comment on the letter appearing . . . [in the previous issue]. The person was upset by the amount private agencies are charging for adoptions.

Name Withheld suspects that $15 per hour should cover the cost of the time the social worker spends with the family. Has [this person] thought about the cost to the agency of training the worker, keeping her abreast of current practices, supervising her, and paying her travel time and mileage to and from a family's home? Has he thought about the time she spends checking references, completing forms, composing the study, then proofing and checking for accuracy? A good worker spends many, many hours on a study beyond those she spends with the family and a good agency invests heavily in its workers' training and supervision.

Agencies must balance their resources in order to provide post-placement services when problems occur. If sufficient fees have not been charged in advance, when problems . . . occur, the agency does not have the resources to provide the intensive post-placement support needed. . . .

For adoptive parents who care about kids beyond those they hope to adopt themselves, there is much that can be done to help agencies keep fees down and provide support services. A few ideas include:

•Raise funds to be used as a revolving loan fund for families adopting children with special needs. (Don't expect agencies to absorb this cost; it will result in higher fees for everyone.)

•Volunteer your time at your agency.

•Help your agency in its fund-raising activities.

•Participate in adoptive parent "hot line" programs to provide support to families having problems.

•Keep unnecessary calls to your agency to a minimum. These are expensive and keep the workers from getting their work done.

By working cooperatively, rather than making accusations, it is possible for agencies and adoptive parents to work together to provide the needed quality services at the lowest possible cost.

Sincerely,
Merrily Ripley

The majority of those working in adoption today, both domestic and foreign, are doing so because their hearts are in the right place. They want to help both the children, who desperately need a family, and the parents who wait with aching empty arms. Prospective parents must be careful. But they also must realize that, like everything else, adoption costs money—sometimes lots of it. Reliable, reputable adoption agencies and advisers will gladly justify their expenses.

Prospective parents must do their part, too, in helping to prevent abuse of the system. In addition to the suggestions given by these two agency directors, they should refuse to patronize those who will not prove themselves to be trustworthy. Adoption is a partnership. If all parties involved work together, the parents, the agency, and, most of all, the children will all come out winners.

9

What about friends and relatives who are against adoption?

*F*ew situations are more disheartening to one who hopes to adopt than to become enthusiastic about the prospect and then, when turning to a parent or valued friend to share the joyous news, to receive a verbal slap in the face. "Why in the world do you want to do *that?* You want to adopt (choose one): someone else's kid? a stranger's child? a foreigner? a crippled kid? a half-grown child? somebody else's mistake?" The prospective adoptive parent, face expectantly aglow, is devastated as the aged twin monsters, ignorance and prejudice, rear their ugly heads once again.

If this same person was sharing news of a pregnancy, the comments would be equally uniform ("Congratulations! That's wonderful! Great!") but because lack of information about adoption and its true nature is still prevalent, many people react in a totally unforeseen manner to the news of a forthcoming adoption.

Fortunately for prospective parents and their waiting children, there is a remedy for this plight, much of which is directly caused by different perceptions of adoption.

The prospective parent should analyze the entire situation carefully before making any moves or sudden announcements. People do not usually spring babies or the news of impending birth on their friends and relatives, except in the movies or on television. A woman is quite obviously pregnant for months, giving all persons affected—herself, her husband, and her extended family members and friends—time to adjust to the idea. People are not conditioned to respond calmly to sudden lifestyle changes. They need time to alter their perception of a twosome into a threesome (or more). The wait in adoption, like the wait in pregnancy, can be a blessing in disguise.

Before a couple announces their intention to adopt a particular type of child, they might casually and impersonally mention adoption and sound out their family's opinion on the subject. Many older family members, such as prospective grandparents and great-grandparents, view adoption as it existed 20 or 30 years ago. They may remember adoption as something cloaked in secrecy, a dark family secret, or a skeleton in the closet. Unless they are unusually well educated on the subject, their only current point of reference may be TV movies or soap opera images of a seemingly impudent teenager searching for biological parents, a blackmail situation, or some equally negative impression. Those faced with the concept of foreign adoption may be at an even greater loss for any tangible connection to their own lives. Their misgivings may include:

(1) *Fear of the unknown.* Not knowing anything of the adopted child's past or personal history is a frightening prospect to many relatives and friends. One adoptive mother was cautioned by a well-meaning friend who was deeply concerned about the young mother raising her biological

daughter, who was a toddler, with her newly adopted infant son!

(2) *End of the family line.* Many people still attach great import to the family bloodline and feel this is the only proof of true family. Some, especially older people, view adoption as a threat to the family ancestral line. The sad side of such a belief is that the daily newspaper proves quite regularly how false it is. Blood is no guarantee of anything.

Almost everyone knows of (or is related to) a family in which the children are born of the same two parents and yet one or more will become upstanding considerate adults while another child of the same union becomes a violent person, a criminal, drug addict, or acts in other irresponsible ways that break the parents' hearts. Biological children offer no better or worse guarantee to their parents than adopted ones, of becoming caring, concerned, responsible adults.

(3) *Fear or prejudice against certain types of children.* Many individuals feel that to raise a child "properly" a parent must adopt a child as an infant or toddler. Such people are often prejudiced and afraid of adopting older children. Others are fearful of children with handicaps. Still others, for one reason or another, fear persons of another race or culture and are uncomfortable with the idea of foreign adoption. For instance, one prospective grandfather whose memories of war in Southeast Asia were quite painful felt tiny Asian faces of Korean grandchildren would leave him forever haunted by guilt.

(4) *Singles should marry first.* A growing number of single persons are becoming adoptive parents and this by itself can be upsetting to their relatives. Old stereotypes are hard to break. Most of society still thinks in terms of marriage first and children later. A prospective grandmother may see the adoption of children by her daughter (or son) as one more

impediment to her eventual marriage. (And despite equal rights and women's lib, most parents do still prefer to see their grown children married and settled after a time.)

The prospective grandmother may also worry about her single daughter becoming a parent and the increased responsibilities involved. She may remember her own difficulties in adjusting to motherhood and *she* had a helpmate. How will her daughter manage alone?

The list of objections is as diversified as the individuals involved in adoption today. Hopefully, prospective parents will realize that it is misplaced fears, misconceptions, and concern for their own welfare that usually sparks such responses.

Prospective parents need not let such negative feedback deter them from their goal of adoption. If a lack of current information and unjustified fears underlie a prospective grandparent's or friend's negative attitude toward adoption, prospective adoptive parents can do something about it.

A number of excellent books are available on specific aspects of adoption. Prospective adoptive parents might select one or two of these which explain the type of adoption they are considering. The wise prospective parent will look the book over carefully to make certain it carries the appropriate message he wants to communicate to the unyielding family member. Such a book should acknowledge the real challenges in the specific type of adoption, but it should also bring those challenges into proper balance with the joys and benefits that come to those who choose the type of adoption in question. A smaller, more personal account may be of more help than a large professional-style volume.

Prospective parents should also try to find pictures of the type of child they hope to adopt if they are not immediately able to secure pictures of their own waiting child. It is difficult for many persons to imagine (1) older children, except for the neighborhood bully or threatening teens seen at the shopping center or on TV; or (2) handicapped children, except one seen in a public place who did not make a good impression. Pictures of these children which give a positive image—handicapped youngsters smiling, playing games, building with blocks, and other normal child activities or pictures of teens helping out in the community, teaching youngsters to swim, or helping elderly persons in a nursing home can help unfounded fears to fade away.

The only mental picture of a foreign child some relatives or friends may call to mind may be the stark black-and-white poster that appeals for funds for overseas relief. While that child may be a pathetic sad-faced underfed waif dressed in rags, he is not what most future grandparents envision when they dream of grandchildren. Pictures of laughing Latin children encircling a piñata or happy Korean children celebrating in traditional costumes can go a long way toward relieving the vague undefined misgivings many prospective grandparents feel at the mention of foreign grandchildren.

Prospective adoptive parents should also share adoptive parent organization newsletters and literature with those they love. In this way, they can learn together and enjoy the photos and stories of children who are already "home to stay" with their adoptive families. The discussions that arise from such current adoption material can help all to better understand one another's feelings about adoption. One adoptive great grandmother, age 75, who lives over 200 miles from her granddaughter's family and her foreign adopted grandson, is a dues-paying member of the adoptive parent support group in her granddaughter's town. She enjoys receiving the quarterly newsletter and takes pleasure in supporting the organization.

If at all possible, prospective parents should take their parents and friends along to an adoptive parent support group meeting. These organizations are open to all persons interested in adoption. In more than one instance, friends who went along to see "what it's all about" eventually became adoptive parents themselves. Seeing other families, meeting the parents and their children, and talking with them could be the most reassuring experience prospective parents can provide for their friends and relatives who are uncertain about adoption.

The basic principle behind all of these suggestions is that prospective parents need to share what they have learned with other family members and close friends so that they too can become excited about adoption. Prospective parents also need to share with others in their community. This is especially true if they are adopting a child who is different than most in the community (a foreign child or a biracial child, for instance). By advance planning and sharing, prospective parents will know where they stand with others. There is no rule that says all must approve of the impending adoption, but it helps to know most of the community is supportive of the effort. And it certainly can help smooth the future son or daughter's entry into the community.

If prospective parents fear (after some time and educational endeavors) that the majority of their family, friends, or neighbors is not behind their plans for adoption, they will be faced with some very difficult decisions.

With the community, it is in some ways easier. The director of a well-known Eastern adoption agency once belted that solution across the room when the question was put to her by a prospective parent at a national adoption convention. *"Move!"* was her one word answer. And that is a solution if attempts to educate the community at large fail. If prospective parents truly feel their new son or daughter will not be accepted, they must consider either moving or trying to adopt a different type of child. It is sad but true that some communities still will not accept a biracial or foreign adopted child. Encouragingly, other areas are ready to change.

Adoptive Parents of the Ozarks, a rural adoptive parent support group in Missouri, began in 1980 when the adoptive mother of a Korean daughter met the adoptive mother of a Central American son. The little boy's adoption was the first foreign adoption ever finalized in that county. The little girl's parents moved to the area after adopting their daughter. They are now far from the only two foreign adopted children in the area, thanks in part to the efforts of the organization their parents founded. Today there are several adopted children from Korea, India, Colombia, Mexico, and El Salvador living nearby. This community was ready to move, to learn, and to grow, and these families were willing to take on that challenge.

Many prospective grandparents and other family members remain unconvinced that this new venture will not cause serious problems, despite educational efforts on the part of the prospective parents. Not until a living, breathing child comes into their lives are they able to begin to relax. One prospective mother could not understand her mother-in-law's concern and foreboding attitude as she and her husband awaited the placement of a foreign baby boy. She knew her mother-in-law adored all children, yet she could sense the grandmother-to-be was not happy about the situation.

Once the bouncing baby boy arrived, however, Grandma was delighted and even scolded another family member who was less than overjoyed at the child's arrival. As the little boy made his adjustment to his new family, the mother-in-law revealed that she had been worried her son and his wife would adopt a sickly child, who would consume their energy for months to come. Once the child arrived and she saw how groundless her fears were, she was able to relax and enjoy life with her new grandson. In the vast majority of cases, once the child arrives, the fear and worries gradually disappear.

In a rare case, however, they do not. Prospective parents should discuss this possibility and decide *in advance* how to handle the situation should it occur. Sometimes a family member will maintain a hostile attitude about adoption and the adopted child. If this happens, the adoptive parents are obligated to take decisive action. Children have a fundamental right to protection by their parents. Obviously, the biological parents were unable to provide such an environment or the child would not be available for adoption. The child does not need another parent who cannot or will not meet his basic needs.

A child's basic needs include protection from emotional and psychological hurts, as well as protection from physical harm. Prejudice, whether for real or imagined reasons, by members of the family, friends, or others welcomed into the family's home can do great harm to the child. If a grandparent or other person cannot treat the child in an appropriately loving manner, parents *must* protect their child by whatever means necessary, including asking the offending party not to visit their home. This may seem a drastic measure and yet when one considers the long-term effects on children who are forced to endure abuse (whether physical, verbal, or psychological), it is the least any caring parent should do.

One family with several foreign adopted children was

forced to a showdown with a grandparent when several years later the adoptive mother gave birth to the only biological grandchild. The grandmother rained presents, affection, and attention on the new grandbaby and studiously ignored the other children in the family. The mother and father each pointed out this offensive behavior to the grandmother on separate occasions but it did not stop. Finally, the parents told the grandmother she would no longer be welcome in their home to visit *any* of their children until she could treat *all* their children in a fair and equitable manner.

It was a big step and a risky one, but it worked. A few weeks later, Grandmama returned, her ways mended. She took time to pay attention to each child and brought presents only when she could do so for every child.

Fortunately, few families ever reach such a crisis point, but it is a possibility that must be considered by all prospective adoptive parents. As our most precious gift, we owe our children the best protection we can possibly provide, or we cannot truly call ourselves loving, caring parents.

10

Should we try foster parenting first?

Cora and her husband, Ed, have been foster parents for 13 years. They became foster parents after their three grown children left home. They have dealt with all kinds of social workers, all sorts of biological and adoptive parents, and have had 13 foster children in their home over the years, seven of whom are still living with them. They live on a farm in the country where the children can play outdoors, learn the responsibilities of farm life, and grow up around living, growing things, both animals and crops.

Cora, whose quick smile and active lifestyle belie her 61 years, looked slightly horrified when asked, "Should prospective adoptive parents try foster parenting before they adopt?"

"Why in the world would they want to?" Cora responded. "When you take in a foster child, you know your time with him will be short. You feel like you need to do as much for the child as you can as soon as possible. Many times you are the first person ever to take him for a complete medical physical or the first ever to take him to the dentist. With adoption you'd have more time to move into these things slowly. With foster care, you don't. He may be gone tomorrow.

"In foster care, you have to deal with the child's biological family—his parents, grandparents, and any other relatives that get involved, plus the agency," Cora explained. "In adoption, you don't have all that family to contend with.

"Your expectations are different, too," she continued. "There's a different kind of bonding that goes on with you and your foster kids. You know from the beginning that you will have to let them go one day soon and that it will hurt. Your expectations are different from those of an adoptive parent. You know from the start that the child comes to you with lots of problems. Like as not, he blames you for his placement in your home. He doesn't blame his folks. He blames you, the stranger. It gets worse when his folks tell him they're coming for a visit or will bring him presents and they don't. Then you have the child's disappointment to handle, too. Worse yet is when they tell their child, 'I'm going to get you back.' The child thinks they mean tomorrow or the next day. The parents are talking of months or even years later, but they don't tell the child that.

"Sometimes the child's parents resent you too and try to turn the child against you," Cora said. "They get scared, I guess, thinking the child will love the foster parents and not love them anymore. Sometimes as a foster parent you find yourself resenting the parents, especially if they are trying to turn the child against you. You wonder if they aren't tearing down all the work you put into that child."

One of the seven children currently living in Cora's home bursts into the kitchen. Mitchell, age 9, has had emotional problems. Cora said when he first came to their home at age

3 he spoke only four words. He struggled even now to form his words as he asked Cora's permission to watch television. "No," she told him, "go outside and ride bikes with Robert. It's a beautiful day."

"Okay," he said, but he didn't move. He turned to the interviewer, asked her name, and attempted to start a conversation with her. His speech was thick and difficult to understand but his smile was quick and spontaneous and the bright eyes alert, a striking contrast to the garbled speech. Robert, also age 9, came in from the school bus, lunch pail and books in hand.

Cora greeted him and then told them both, "Outside, outside." They tumbled and scuffled out the kitchen door as only 9-year-old boys can. Cora continued, "Each child comes with different troubles because each child handles his problems differently. Many times you don't know what the problems are. After a child has been with you awhile, you start to find out!" She laughed softly.

"And if you think you've got paperwork and red tape with adoption, you should see it in foster care! Forms to sign, court hearings to attend, social workers, juvenile officers, court officials, lawyers—everybody wants a piece of you and this child."

She stopped for a moment to catch her breath. "Sounds pretty awful, doesn't it?" She smiled. "And some days it is."

"Why?" the interviewer asked. "Why do you keep doing it?"

Cora's smile broadened, her voice softened, and her eyes shone brightly. Her gruff manner eased a bit. "When you see a child in your home for the first time, wandering around, you suddenly realize yours is the first real home he has ever been in. You know you are giving him a chance he may never have again—a chance to see what his life *could*

be like if he is willing to go after it. Your family may be the
first real family he's ever been with.

"One of my foster kids asked one day, 'Why don't you
have a boyfriend and why doesn't Dad have a girlfriend?'
Now what does that tell you about his former family life?
When you realize you are giving the children something no
one else ever has, and maybe never will again, you know it's
worth it. I really can't explain it any better than that. I guess
we do it just because we love children. We really do. I've
told these kids, 'I've had all the pains a mother can have
with every one of you. The only thing I haven't had with
you is the birthin' pains and the ownin' pains, but I've had
all the rest.' "

Red-haired Julie walked with difficulty across the kitchen
to where Cora was sitting. The awkward gait and disjointed
arm movements identified her as a child with cerebral palsy,
but she attends public school with the boys. She asked her
foster mother about when she will next see her biological
mother. "We've already talked this all through," Cora told
her patiently. "Not this weekend but the next."

Julie frowned and insisted in slurred tones that tomorrow
is the day she has been waiting for.

"Not tomorrow, next weekend," Cora repeated firmly
and patted her hand. Julie gave the interviewer an irritated
glance and continued to shake her head. Her mother told
her to go do her homework and she reluctantly obeyed.

As she moved slowly away, the interviewer asked quietly
about her age. "About 8?"

"No, she's 12, but quite small for her age, isn't she?" Cora
said fondly, still watching Julie continue on her way.

"We worry when they go back. There are a lot of mixed,
jumbled-up feelings. Is this the best move for them? Will
they be okay or will they be back again in a few weeks or

months and just as troubled as when we first saw them? And we also wonder if we will ever see them again." She sighed and was silent for a few moments, lost in her own private thoughts.

"To be a good foster parent you need to know your own limitations," Cora said. "What kinds of kids you can work with best. There are handicapped children, teenagers, and of course babies." Cora's face broke into a special smile. "We do love babies here," she added a little self-consciously. "Foster parents need to know what kind of child they can care for best."

"What about people who claim foster parents are in it for the money?" the interviewer asked.

The fire snapped back into Cora's eyes as she nearly spit out the distasteful words. "That's the worst, most hurtful thing you can say about a foster parent. It's so ridiculous! Do you know in this state the highest foster care payment is less than $200 a month? And that's for a teenager. Have you ever tried to help them have a chance at the things others their age have on less than $200 a month? Things like nice blue jeans, a class yearbook, school pictures, school jacket, team sports and uniforms, their own transportation, school supplies, and a little spending money of their own?

"Forget it! For the little kids, the monthly payment's even less than that. A lot of times the child comes through your door with nothing but the clothes he has on. You've got shoes to buy, clothes, all sorts of things. And you don't get mileage either for all the trips to town [16 miles one way in Cora's case] or to the city [50 miles past the town] for counseling and special treatments. One of the kids had braces on her teeth and we had plenty of trips last summer to get those adjusted."

Cora laughed. "It's got to be done, though. So," she

shrugged, "what are you going to do? It's plain that anybody who says foster parents are in it for the money, doesn't know anything about foster parenting. It costs you in a lot of ways to be a foster parent." She sighed.

"But we'll keep doing it as long as we're able." She nodded her head toward the other room where several children could be heard talking, laughing, and squabbling. "Because more important than all the hassles and money is the fact that they need us. It's as simple as that."

As the interview ended, another child came in, this one from high school. She had been on the telephone with a girlfriend and began to tell her mother of some great injustice that took place that day at school. Cora listened quietly.

"I'm not going to do it, that's all!" her eldest foster child exploded.

"Well, you don't have to," her mother responded calmly. "She's another student just like you and you don't have to do her bidding."

The young woman relaxed as relief spread across her face. "Good," she said in much calmer tones. "Because I really don't want to." She smiled her thanks to Cora.

"Fine," said her mother. "Don't worry about it anymore then. Why don't you help me start dinner?"

Since foster care is seen as a poor substitute for a permanent home, whether with the biological family or an adoptive family, it often goes unappreciated for what it *does* provide. Most foster parents provide homes for children at all hours of the day and night. They feed, clothe, shelter, and most of all, love children who frequently see the foster parents as the cause of their dilemma rather than the answer to it. Children are shuttled in and out of foster homes many times like so many packages, and delivery often as not is at 3:00 a.m. with the child in question bringing nothing with him but the dirty clothes or pajamas he is wearing.

Some foster parents are not as dedicated as Cora and her husband. A few eventually abuse the children in their care, and some try to get by on what the state pays and the children suffer the consequences, but they are a tiny minority. Most foster parents, like Cora and Ed, end up plowing a large portion of their own financial resources into the children's care.

Another foster parent had a different viewpoint concerning foster care payments. "If you see the monthly payments as only a reimbursement plan, you'll have trouble from the outset. We've always considered the payments as a help, a supplement to the care we provide. That way we don't get so upset when it doesn't cover many of the expenses." This is a positive and highly optimistic outlook but maybe it comes closer to explaining how and why many foster parents continue on a minimal amount of money.

Although Cora never stated it in so many words, the message is there for those who can read between the lines. The difference for some persons between foster parenting and adoptive parenting is a question of needs. Cora and Ed, like many others who continue to foster parent for a number of years, have already had their own needs as parents satisfied. Having raised three biological children, their own parenting needs have been met by these children. For this reason, they have the ability to continue to give of themselves to their foster children. They even have several grandchildren older than most of their foster children.

For others, however, the foster parenting experience leads to adoption. Agencies are increasingly looking to foster parents as an adoptive resource, as a way of eliminating additional losses in a child's life.

The great danger for most prospective adoptive parents

who become involved in foster parenting is that their own unmet needs will eventually undermine any good they may be able to do. People who adopt do so to help a child but also to satisfy their own desires to love, nurture, and raise a child. There is nothing particularly wrong or selfish in these desires. They are perfectly normal and natural.

In many cases, however, children are reluctant or unable to return a parent's affections for a long time. The reasons are many. Children with severe emotional problems cannot always love others. Children who have changed homes many times may no longer trust anyone enough to dare to love them. They feel it will only bring them heartache in a short while when they are forced to move on again. Their refusal to love is a self-protection measure that they have learned in the original school of hard knocks. Some children may interpret affection for their foster parents as being disloyal to their biological or alternate parents. Other children may blame their substitute parents for their predicament of changing homes, lifestyle, and environment.

Parents who do not have other children who can provide the love and affection they themselves need, may quickly wear out as foster parents. These children, like other older special needs children (see chapter 1), can usually be helped when they are permanently placed in a home. It is this question of permanency that makes much of the difference for a child between a foster home and an adoptive home. And so it is also with the parents. Many prospective adoptive parents can tell their social worker (and themselves) that they are prepared to keep a child temporarily while they wait for that special (adoptable) child; however, telling and doing and living are very different things indeed.

One social worker characterized the foster parents she had worked with in this way. "Foster parents are great. They give their best to the kids and often get the worst that the agency has to offer in the way of support. For all that they give, they might get a dinner once a year given in their honor by the agency to say thanks. For all that they do, it's hardly enough. I hope they know that they are loved, respected, and appreciated. In a lot of places, they are simply used and abused, until they burn out and just can't give any more. That's the real tragedy of foster care."

Historically, foster care and adoption have been seen as separate spheres of the same field—parenting in the child welfare system. At times they intersected, but they often seemed to have more differences than similarities. There are parents who can successfully combine the two. But new or prospective parents who are sure that adoption is their goal are advised not to consider foster parenting a sure path to adoption. Caution in this regard is simply easier on the hearts of all concerned.

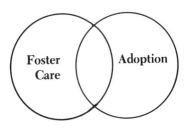

Parenting in the Child Welfare System

11

Why are there so many different kinds of adoption?

(Private agency, private, transracial, legal risk, open, cross-cultural, and independent adoptions)

*R*ecent television programs and movies have depicted attractive children of a century ago on New York orphan trains headed west, in frontier orphanages, and in similar imaginative but unrealistically romanticized situations. Such shows may provide a relatively harmless evening of light entertainment. They may also help to deepen the shock of persons today who continue to view adoption as a simple process, as they move into an unfamiliar world of confusing jargon, overworked social workers, and harried public officials—known as adoption in modern America.

Many still perceive adoption as hopeful parents going to the local agency or orphanage, filling out a few forms, and after a short wait, receiving a child to raise and love. It sounds nice, but it no longer works that way, if indeed it ever actually was that simple and straightforward.

There are few, if any, true orphanages left in America today. Most homeless, neglected, destitute children are actually cared for in foster homes. This makes them much less visible and more difficult to track and monitor as a group or as individuals. Many children live in group homes and residential treatment facilities. Far too many are housed in homes/institutions that were designed for the mentally retarded, emotionally disabled, or the severely physically disabled, rather than for children with families who are unable or unwilling to care for them. Nonetheless, the majority of these children are not and will never be available for adoption. Many will eventually return to the home of their parents or another relative. Others will remain in group home situations until they can move out on their own, but a growing number will be in need of another permanent home through adoption.

New prospective parents are often shocked to discover that adoption is a multi-faceted topic. There are not only many types of children available for adoption, there is also a seemingly endless variety of ways parents may choose to bring children into their lives. The jargon may be confusing in the beginning and ambiguous at times since even the terminology changes from place to place. Certain adoptions may also fall into more than one category. Still, the practices remain basically the same as prospective adoptive parents search for new and creative ways to bring today's lost children home—to loving permanent families.

Following are descriptions and explanations of seven of the most common types of adoption taking place across America today.

Private Agency. Most children who are adopted in the United States are placed for adoption by an agency, either public or private. The public agency is usually a state agency, but is dependent upon local county offices for daily operation. The local office is most often located in or near the family/child welfare office and its performance in adoptions may rate anywhere from exceptionally good to abysmal and inoperative. This diversity is not only found from state to state, but many times from county to county, and from area to area within a single state.

Like public agencies, private agencies run the gamut from excellent to appalling in the quality of service they provide. With both, prospective parents may find frustration with red tape and long waits. But with a private agency they are paying for the privilege, as opposed to the public agency which is supported, wholly or in part, by tax dollars.

Included are private agencies which on occasion place American infants, private agencies connected to a particular religious denomination, private agencies that place foreign children, and the latest development, private agencies that place special needs American children.

Private agencies are subject to the laws and licensing procedures of their own state, which in itself accounts for a great deal of the diversity of private agency procedures. Some may be licensed to place children only in their own state or metropolitan area while others work with prospective adoptive parents in an entire region or a large number of states.

Years ago, private agencies generally placed newborn infants and many operated a home for unwed mothers in conjunction with the adoption services they offered. There were even a few chain operations, large foundations which maintained several such homes and adoption agencies in a number of states. With society's more relaxed attitude toward children born outside of marriage, fewer young girls feel the need for a place to hide away such as these homes offered and very few of them are still in operation today (see chapter 2).

Currently, a number of church organizations place children for adoption, but their waiting lists are long and their fees are high. Generally they will place children only with couples of their specific religious faith. There are a few exceptions, however, and the only way for prospective parents to know which agency adheres to which policies is to inquire.

The private agencies placing the most children today are those who specialize in foreign adoption. These agencies may place children from only one country (as is the practice of many of the Korean placement agencies) or they may place children from a number of countries. To place children from a particular country, an agency must have one or more persons working with them or for them in the foreign country. This might be a social worker, an attorney, or other contact. An agency that loses its contact person may have to cease operation in the country in question if it is unable to secure an appropriate replacement. In a few instances, as is the case with some of the older more established adoption agencies, there may be a full agency staff operating in the foreign country. Still, due to the capricious nature of some foreign governments, a private agency's activities in any particular country can be sharply curtailed or terminated at a moment's notice.

Most private agencies, like most persons working in adoption, do so to help others and to continue to serve the children involved, the parents, and the community at large. There are exceptions, however, and parents should be careful and research the agency they choose thoroughly (see chapters 7 and 8).

A recent development is the agency that places special needs American children. In the past, this has been the principal domain of the public service agency. But as prospective parents have become discouraged with the poor work being done in many public service agencies across the country, this new sort of private agency has sprung up, offering hope to those who want to adopt American children but who were unable to do so through the public agency.

In several cases, these special needs agencies charge moderate fees, which many times are scaled to prospective parents' income. They make excellent use of such developments as adoption exchange resource books. Their staff of professional social workers are able to secure more information on a child in another region or state than the average prospective parent. Child placements that are made from one state or another are often facilitated through such an agency. Relinquishing mothers are also likely to choose a private agency, feeling they and their child will receive more personalized service than they might at the public agency.

One of the most promising changes in years in adoption has come through private agencies. An item that is cropping up in a number of public agency budgets is something called *purchase of service.* Several states with commendable foresight have begun to budget monies to pay private agencies through purchase of service (p.o.s.) agreements to search out loving homes for children with exceptional special needs or children who have spent more time than usual on state and regional adoption exchanges, waiting for a home. This includes older black teenage young men, older handicapped boys of all races, and many children with severe disabilities.

Private or Privately Arranged Adoptions. "The three private individuals most likely to be contacted when a couple begins to search for an adoptable infant are the local doctor, minister/priest/rabbi, or attorney," says the president of a large adoptive parent support group. "Unfortunately, these same individuals may know little more than the inquiring couple. Occasionally, these persons are called upon to actually arrange a private adoption but due to their gross lack of experience in the field, it is a risky business for all involved.

"A lawyer is not usually in a position, for example, to provide or even direct his clients, both the adopting and the relinquishing parents, to appropriate emotional counseling, if it is needed. Doctors and clergy may not be properly informed about the legal aspects of adoption, and none are truly prepared for the enormous task of acting as go-between the two sets of parents in today's adoption system.

"On the other hand, they are often in a position to at least investigate the matter to some extent or to know who the best local contact might be for general adoption information. For this reason, we often send our organization's newsletter to our community's lawyers, churches, and medical clinics."

Depending on the state, private adoptions may or may not be legal and the term "private adoption" may include a number of forms of adoption. These are non-agency American adoptions which include no social work professional involvement and have been the most vulnerable to abuse. In the state of New Jersey, for instance, the term private adoption refers to a form of adoption in which the biological mother relinquishes her child directly to the adopting couple. It is illegal there for an attorney, a doctor, or other third party to act as a go-between, passing the child from the biological mother to the adoptive parents. In an occasional case, this sort of adoption might take place when a child is adopted by another family member, such as an aunt or a grandparent.

In several Midwestern states, private adoptions may be arranged through a lawyer, a doctor, or other private individual. They are often referred to as "gray adoptions," for while they are not blatantly illegal, they are not heartily approved of by either the courts or professional social work agencies.

Little or no legal protection is afforded the adopting parents as they go through this process. They may trustingly agree, for instance, to pay a young unmarried girl's medical bills, and do so, as she gives birth to a baby. Even so, if the new mother changes her mind and decides to keep her baby, the prospective parents have little or no recourse. Even if the young mother has signed papers to relinquish the child, many judges will allow her to reclaim her child 30 days or more later. Most judges and many others continue to believe that birth makes a stronger bond than adoption, a hotly contested issue. In such a situation, the prospective parents usually lose not only the child but whatever they paid to cover the mother's expenses and any fees paid to the third party involved. (The young mother is also at risk since if her child is born with any disabilities, the adopting parents may change their minds and refuse to accept the child, thus leaving her with a handicapped child she never intended to raise.)

In one almost bizarre case, a prospective adoptive mother desperate to adopt an infant stood outside an abortion clinic in a major city trying to dissuade the young women entering and to find one who might allow her to adopt her yet unborn child. One young girl who refused to reconsider her decision stated flatly, "I already have one child at home I can't afford and don't want. Why should I have another?" She kept her appointment for the abortion that day but the prospective mother was able to adopt the girl's 18-month-old daughter a few months later. The prospective mother took a great risk, making contacts as she did. While it is certainly not a recommended practice, she did find a child to adopt.

Not all are so lucky, however. Abuses of the private adoption system are not only dangerous for the adults involved but also for the young lives who are involuntarily shuttled from one family to another. Kidnapped or stolen children have on rare occasion been placed by an unethical type, hoping to make quick money in the adoption game. Likewise, individuals working in adoption have grossly overcharged their clients, both the biological mother and the prospective parents, in an attempt to turn adoption into a lucrative sideline. Both of these examples belong to the world of black market adoption.

While most might prefer to believe that such abuses no longer occur, an occasional adopting parent does stumble across this kind of tragic situation. Before dealing in any way with any questionable adoption source, prospective parents should check with their local public service agency, their local adoptive parent support group, or any other reputable adoption organization in the community. Prospective parents, no matter how tempted, should *never* put their faith or their money into an unknown private adoption source if they have no proof of the individual's integrity or reliability. And all parents must remember that to unknowingly become involved in an illegal adoption will eventually bring only many more heartaches to both the adopting parents and the innocent child involved.

Transracial Adoption. In a September 1979 editorial in the *Indianapolis Star*, Roy Wilkins, the respected black leader and spokesman, attempted to answer the question, "What Color Is Love?" (He was responding to a judge's custody decision in a Connecticut court case.) He wrote:

In Connecticut, a court has said that if a black child is in need of parents, the answer is that love comes only in hues of ebony and brown. The judge decided that it would not be in the "best interest" of a 4-month-old black baby to permit its white foster parents to adopt the child, whom they raised since birth. The underlying fear is that the interracial adoption would confuse the child's identity.

Many factors including law, tradition, psychology, politics, and superstition, go into the continuance of such a color-conscious social policy that has the effect of depriving otherwise adoptable black children of a stable, loving family life. The state which permits such archaic considerations as the race of the prospective parents to bar an adoption bears a heavy responsibility for cruelty to children by sending them instead to institutions or passing them from one foster home to the next. It is a social theology which can, and often does, result in tragic situations, with lifetime and deep repercussions.

Racial prejudice among the populace no doubt is a serious problem for any black child. Racism is also a skillful and ruthless adversary bent upon destroying a person's mental health. It is axiomatic that the segregated environment (that arises from racial attitudes among the population) does great harm to the minds and hearts of children in ways unlikely ever to be undone. That goes for white as well as black children.

The task, therefore, is to free individuals in particular and society generally of primitive passions about race. Racial prejudice, discrimination, and segregation are damaging to the human personality, not the love a parent has for its child who is not racially matched.

There is absolutely no valid basis by which a child should be taken away from people who care and love him solely because of his skin pigmentation. A rule of law which requires the separation of the black child and the white foster parents is a sham and a lot of racial nonsense. It is an excuse offered in support of human cruelty under the guise of acting in the child's best interests.

Of course no one, black or white, can grow up in America and not be aware of distinctions made on the basis of one's skin color. But that poses the challenge ahead not the repetition of discredited racism.

The task is that of reeducating the populace, not of mimicking the ignorant. Here, truth about race and racism have critical importance. We must educate, train, and utilize every ounce of courage in our bodies to wipe out the evils of judgment according to skin color.

Racial barriers which have existed must be dissolved. Today we no longer prohibit intermarriage. How, then, can we condemn interracial adoption? In modern times, having parents with lighter or darker skins, or two parents from different cultures and ethnicities, is commonplace. To render a black child "unadoptable" or label his white foster parents "unable" or unfit to adopt him on the grounds of racial incompatibility would be the advice of the segregationist.

We do not need as a law, or as a tradition, an official court pronouncement shunting black children aside when whites come to adopt.°

Perhaps no type of American adoption has sparked more controversy in the past 20 years than transracial adoption—that is, Caucasian parents adopting black children and occasionally, vice versa.

More than 50 percent of the special needs children available for adoption in the United States are black or biracial (in some areas the percentage is even higher) while the vast majority of waiting couples and singles are Caucasian. Black couples who are now adopting are usually young infertile couples seeking black healthy infants or very young children. Older black children, biracial children, and black children with handicaps often find themselves waiting years for a permanent family and many never have a family they can call their own. Yet in most cases when white prospective parents have attempted to step in and fill the gap, the hue and cry raised by social workers and black civil rights organizations has been staggering.

Among the reasons cited are these: "To grow up in a color-conscious world, a child needs parents who are of the

---

°Reprinted courtesy of The Register and Tribune Syndicate, Inc.

same race she is...." "The child will end up caught between two worlds, black on the outside due to birth and white on the inside due to upbringing...." "White parents cannot give a black child the education and psychological defenses he will need to make it in a white world" ... and on and on. Some have even gone so far as to suggest that Caucasian parents would not know how to care for a black child's skin or naturally curly or kinky hair. No matter how profound, how simple, or how ridiculous the justifications and rationalizations become, they are all secondary to a child's need to a permanent home, loving parents, a sense of belonging, loving, and being loved.

No one is suggesting that transracial or interracial adoption, as it is sometimes called, is the ideal arrangement. It would be preferable if all children could be placed with families of a similar background, and toward this end many areas like the state of Georgia have instituted minority family recruitment campaigns. The most famous minority family recruitment project is Detroit's Homes for Black Children, which has been the model for many other major cities' campaigns. Homes for Black Children has proved that many minority families are willing to adopt, provided they feel they will be accepted by the traditional adoption system, which in the past has been all white.

Agencies might well review whether any of their policies make it difficult for blacks to adopt. It has been demonstrated that if an agency includes minority staff, and if they actively recruit in the black community and understand minority families, blacks will come forward to adopt these children. But because of the high percentage of black and biracial children awaiting adoption, even if the blacks absorbed many of these, what would happen to the ones who were left?

Many states are currently in a quandary over this issue as they try to move from old-style policies to new ones that will better serve the children involved. Some states (such as Arkansas) continue to live in the past, declaring that black and biracial children are never to be placed with white families. Other states (such as South Carolina which repealed its law against transracial adoption in 1981) are struggling to move out of past centuries of segregation and prejudice, but are still doing so extremely slowly. Some states (such as Missouri) have a nebulous set of rules composed partly of statutes and partly of policies, both written and unwritten, that is irregularly enforced. A few states (such as Vermont and Idaho) have no policy at all since they have rarely encountered the problem because they have no waiting black children. An attempt was made during the 1980-81 legislative session in California to pass a law against transracial adoption. This demonstrates that while some states are making progress and others are still floundering, a few are actually moving backwards! (The California measure was soundly defeated, in great part due to the efforts and outrage expressed by parents who had adopted transracially and cross-culturally.)

Minnesota, once again, is leading other states with a three-part transracial policy backed by state law. This plan has a 90-day time frame which gives first preference for adoption to members of the child's extended family, second preference to adoptive parents of the same race, and third preference to prospective adoptive parents of another race. However, the law indicates that these parents should be appreciative of the child's racial identity and be able to demonstrate that sensitivity through such practical circumstances as life in a racially mixed community and friends of other races and/or cultures.

Other states that claim to adhere to this or that policy often include no workable timetable or do not enforce the policies they have on the books. Children continue to languish in foster care or institutional care with no real end in sight. The laws and policies that are supposed to help them actually add to the length of foster care stays.

Many black and biracial children find their way into Caucasian families through foster care systems. Many states have laws or rules that specify that foster parents who have had a particular child in their home for more than 12 or 18 months shall have first preference should the child become available for adoption. However, these policies tend to be suspended disproportionately often when the child involved is black or biracial. Some states have carried this sort of policy to such extremes as to insist that all biracial children, even a child that is classified biracial by virtue of a grandparent or other more distant relative, *must* be considered black and therefore, placed in a black home. Such policies enrage moderates, be they black or white, since the fact remains that whether such plans are fomented by white supremists in state legislatures or black urban militants, their source is the same—racism. Biracial children and black children are obviously always going to carry their color and racial features with them but should these attributes be considered an integral part of the child or the singular most important overriding characteristic of the child's life?

It is not a simple issue. Obviously, great care must be taken to find sensitively educated families when transracial adoption is a factor. Yet certainly there must be an alternative other than to resort to the classification of people in an emulation of South Africa's policies. White and black foster families who house, parent, love, nurture, and care for children of another race, greatly resent the government's attitude that while they are "good enough" to provide foster care for the child (often for an open-ended period of time) they are not "good enough" to adopt the child and provide a permanent home for the child they have grown to love.

Legal Risk Adoption. Not only may it be difficult to find a social worker who cares to discuss transracial adoption, it may be almost impossible to find agency personnel who are willing to talk about legal risk adoptions. These are the cases that devastate prospective parents, find social workers resigning in tears and frustration, and leave a child in continuous legal limbo.

A child who is legally at risk is one who is in need of a permanent home, but one whose parental rights, for one reason or another, cannot be terminated. This may come about in a variety of ways. Randy is a classic legal risk child (see chapter 1). Totally ignored and uncared for by both biological parents, he was placed in foster care as an infant. A few years later the state began reviewing all children in the foster care system. They wanted to determine how many could be placed for adoption, returned to a relative's home, or otherwise released from foster care. As a result, the walls began to crash down around this 4-year-old and his single foster mother.

Unlike many children, Randy was not shuffled from one foster home to another. He was placed in one home and it was assumed by both the public agency social workers and his foster mother that he would remain there throughout his youth since his biological mother's whereabouts were unknown and his biological father was totally uninterested in him. As different states have adopted various permanency planning programs to update, rejuvenate, and improve their foster care and adoption programs, some children always seem to fall through the cracks in the new system. It may be considered a necessary evil by some state planners and bu-reaucrats. However, in human terms it is a tragedy for the individual child. Is a program that serves the needs of several thousand children of real value when it ultimately destroys the lives of a few dozen?

In Randy's case, his biological father who resided several hundred miles away in another state was notified that a hearing would soon terminate his parental rights to the child. For the first time in this child's life, his father decided to take an interest in him. For many children, this would have been the end of the story. After one or two preliminary visits, this shy boy raised in a quiet rural Midwestern town would have been separated from the only mother he had ever known and sent to live with a man he had never met and his new wife, who lived in a northern urban area.

The difference in this child's fate was made by the one person who had always made a difference in his life, his foster mother. Sympathetic public agency social workers advised Lorraine that her chances of winning such a case in court were extremely small and that on her moderate in-come a court battle and its ensuing legal fees were best avoided. Still she remained undaunted as she maintained, "He's my son, much more so than anyone else's. I've cared for him, loved him, been there for him. I've *got* to fight for him. That's also a part of being a mother."

She gambled and, much to the delight of all, she won. (The father apparently returning to his old habits was neg-ligent about many details of the case, including paying his lawyer, submitting proper documents when requested, and meeting other demands of the court.)

The father's rights were involuntarily terminated. Not all such cases have a happy ending. Many "true parents"—the foster or adoptive parents, who have cared for, loved, fed, clothed, and nursed a particular child—have walked out of the courtroom stunned as a judge rules in favor of a biological parent or relative, often disregarding all circumstances, save one—who sired or gave birth to the child.

For this reason alone, legal risk cases can be devastating. In many areas, judges will not terminate a biological parent's rights until an adoptive family is found for the child. Social service agencies, however, are often extremely reluctant to involve prospective parents with a child whose life may unexpectedly erupt into an emotional volcano as a formerly uninterested parent suddenly decides to take action. The child then remains in a classic Catch-22 situation. This predicament can and does continue for some children until age 18 when, in most states, they are simply adjudicated and cut loose from the system as Micheal was (see chapter 1).

Increasingly, agencies are looking at legal risk placement as a way of eliminating unnecessary separation. Because the trend is new, however, and the judicial system inconsistent, not all cases end well.

Fortunately, some prospective parents are brave enough and strong enough to take the risks involved. In one case, a newborn infant was relinquished by a young mother but the judge, fearing an attempt might be made later to revoke the termination of parental rights, refused to rule on the relinquishment for 60 days. The baby might have been placed in a foster home, but many agencies are trying to avoid such placements when they know that the child will be moved again in short order. Instead, a young childless couple who had been waiting for some time to adopt decided to gamble. They accepted the baby, knowing full well they might lose her in 60 days when the judge made his ruling known.

The couple's social worker did her best to prepare them for whatever the outcome might be. In part she told them:

"This child is not unlike a child that might come to you with a heart defect or other life-threatening disorder. In 60 days, a professional will operate. If the operation is a success, the baby will live a normal life with you and your family, with no further complications that we can foresee. But should the operation fail, this child will undoubtedly be lost to you forever." This is the reality of legal risk adoption.

The operation was a success as the judge let the termination order stand and the child remains today, (at age 2) with her adoptive parents.

Not all cases are so clean-cut, for just as all medical complications cannot be resolved by an operation, so many legal risk children cannot be easily freed from the system that holds them. In many cases, the biological parents have learned how the court system in their particular area works. They know how much attention they must pay and how many contacts per year they must make with their children to prevent a judge from terminating their parental rights. Literally, hundreds of children in the United States are caught in long-term foster care/legal risk situations. A biological parent may visit the child only once or twice a year and send him an occasional postcard or small toy. All his needs for love and affection, daily care, and material goods are met by someone else—the foster parents, who even if they want to adopt the child and give him a sense of permanency, cannot. The courts will rarely terminate the rights of a parent who makes contacts with their child(ren), even though they are infrequent.

If the comparison might be made again to a child with a serious health problem, these children are similar to children with a serious disease or inoperable disorder. No one knows how long such children will live and/or if their health might return in the years ahead. So is the uncertainty of life with a child caught in legal limbo. The dilemma may not be solvable in the present or the future. While the ideal situation is to be able to give a child a permanent home, foster/ legal risk parents must not forget that they are giving the child something very special and very necessary for healthy, normal growth just by being there for them every day.

One 11-year-old child who was returning to her biological parents' home after five years with another family told her legal risk mother as she left, "I won't forget what you've done for me or what you've taught me. I know when I'm on my own someday, what you've taught me will help me more than anything else I've ever learned in my whole life." Whatever the eventual fate of the child, they will not forget.

The parents of health-impaired children usually learn to live with their insecure situation as it is, and so sometimes must the parents of children caught inextricably in the system. To fall into the pit called self-pity will only tear the entire family to shreds. Counseling and other outside assistance may be needed to help families make their adjustment to this heart-rending situation, but in the long run, they will be the winners in that they gave of themselves to a child when no one else would.

Open adoption. Three biological mothers, upon receiving letters and pictures from their children's adoptive families, responded as follows:

(1) "I sat there and read the letter about ten times. Then I started crying. Not because I was sad but they were tears of happiness. I was so happy because I knew he was healthy and happy."

(2) "I will always cherish these pictures. They in a special way fill an emptiness I feel inside myself every once in a while."

(3) "I'm relieved that she looks so well and happy. It's so

much nicer to see for myself. I'm convinced she's well and normal."°

As greater numbers of adoptive parents have sought more alternatives to traditional secretive white infant adoptions of years past, open adoptions have increased. Open adoption takes place when the adopting parents know the biological parent or parents. It has been happening for years in cases in which the child to be adopted is a niece, nephew, grand-child, or neighbor. Today, in some adoption cases, the bio-logical parent(s) or the adopting parent(s) may specifically request information, photographs, or even the opportunity to meet one another. All these options are often referred to collectively as open adoption.

In the first option, sharing information and photographs, many biological parents who have made the decision to re-linquish a child for adoption are still concerned about the child. They'd like to know how the child is doing, what he looks like, if she is healthy, and so on. Through an agreement formalized by the placement agency, adoptive parents can send letters and pictures, usually on a yearly basis, to help ease the biological parent's anxieties and let her know the child is progressing well.

Some adoptive parents and biological parents may find such an arrangement too intrusive or painful. But it can be quite satisfying for others, as expressed in the remarks of the relinquishing biological mothers quoted above. Adoptive parents' comments also show they have found such sharing agreements to be a satisfactory arrangement.

> Adoptive parents have expressed appreciation and satisfac-
> tion in choosing to have an opportunity to share their "pride

---

°From "Options in Adoption," in a report by Carol Sorich, published by the Child Saving Institute of Omaha, Nebraska.

and joy" with the birth parents. They have expressed pleasure in being able to reassure the birth parents of the happiness and health of their child and in being given increased opportunities for contact with the birth parent. [Two] of these families have discussed their thoughts and feelings about sharing [below]:

(1) " . . . We know that if we were in her shoes, we would want to view pictures just to see if the baby was alive and looked happy and healthy. . . . We find it a small token of our appreciation for what she did, to share some pictures with her. We find the most difficult thing about sharing pictures is picking out the pictures to send. . . . Much love and care goes into the selection of that special picture. . . . Our family (grandparents, etc.) enjoys helping us to get the baby to smile really big for the camera for that special picture."

(2) " . . . There are several specific reasons for our willingness to share pictures/information. The ones that strike us as being most important are sharing pride, thankfulness, reassurance, and the baby's future. What more could anyone share with us? Adoption itself is probably the greatest form of sharing there is. . . . Our pride in him bursts out at the seams all the time. . . . Sharing a picture is just a reflection of that pride. We are so thankful to have him that any small means of repaying the person who made it possible for our lives to be so complete is so little to ask of us. . . . To reassure her that he's okay makes us feel good. We think that the baby will have a better understanding of our feelings about adoption if he knows eventually that we were open about *sharing* him. The most important thing after all is his happiness."[∘]

In the second choice, semi-open adoption, a meeting may be arranged between the biological mother and the adoptive parents. This arrangement can work wonders for the biological parent who can be greatly reassured by meeting the people who will be adopting her child. It can also be helpful to the adopting parents, giving them the opportunity to ask questions directly and secure whatever information they might need, including family medical information. It makes

---

[∘] Ibid.

it easier for the adopting parents to feel comfortable about the biological parents. It is easier in turn to communicate clearly, without ambivalence, positive impressions of the parents to the adopted child. Responses by parents, both biological and adoptive, affirm the benefits of such contact.

> "I bet if there was a lot more people like Ann and Joe, there would be a lot more happier unwed mothers, knowing their baby is alright. I'm so glad you [agency personnel] found them for me. I really don't worry that much knowing that they are taking care of her."
>
> The adoptive mother's response:
>
> "We feel that this type of adoption was extremely helpful in that we know a little about the mother and the father's background that we can tell [our daughter] when she is old enough to understand. We can also explain how hard it was for her mother to give her up.... She decided to relinquish only out of the love she has for her daughter.... By meeting her, it has answered many of the questions we would always have. In our next adoption, if there is any, I hope we can meet with the mother."[*]

In semi-open adoption, identifying information (such as complete names and addresses) is not shared and the parties involved meet at a neutral location, such as the adoption agency's office. In this way, neither may recontact the other at a later date, except through the agency.

Fully open adoption takes place when the adopting parents and the biological parents know one another. Foster parents are familiar with this type of adoption and have been for years. Under this arrangement it is not unusual for the biological parent(s) to visit their child in the foster family's home. If after a time, the foster parents are able to adopt the child, they do so in an open adoption, often hav-

---

[*] Ibid.

ing met many times with the biological parent(s).

In a few cases special arrangements have even been made for the expectant mother to live near or with the adopting parents so that they may have an extended time to know each other and share information and feelings about adoption. Such situations are arranged through private organizations, agencies, or individuals. Occasionally there are other situations when it is important for the biological parent to meet the adopting parent. One black adoptive mother sought out her children's biological father in his neighborhood as she was in the process of adopting three siblings. This was not the usual search for a biological parent through court records and old documents. This was an adoptive mother who felt a need to talk with the father of her adopted children so that she could better understand her children's adjustment and help to ease them through this tumultuous time in their lives.

In many cases of open adoption, social workers prefer to secure specific agreements between biological parents and adopting parents regarding visitation rights and other expectations and restrictions for all parties involved. The end result can more than pay for the complicated intricacies sometimes involved, as expressed by one family:

> "We want our children to grow up with an openness to others, whatever the race, handicap, or difference of opinion may be. We feel that living this way will enrich their lives. It seems only natural that we would welcome our adopted child's birth parents into our home and family. He exists because they gave him life and nurtured him until his birth. We think of them as relatives. No family can be too large. No one can have too much love."

Cross-cultural Adoption. This term is often used synonymously with foreign adoption and/or transracial adoption. Sometimes they are the same, but not in all cases. Technically, there are but three races of humans—Caucasian, Negroid, and Mongoloid (simplified figuratively, if erroneously, as white, black, and yellow). All peoples fall into one of the three, yet many cultural and even religious groups are often referred to by race, such as the Jewish race or the Indian race (meaning either Native Americans or Asians).

Even if one accepts the idea that there are only three races, there is still a great amount of diversity among Caucasian people (Europeans, Latin Americans, American and Asian Indians), Negroid peoples (all blacks from Africa, the Caribbean nations, North America), and Mongoloid peoples (all Koreans, Chinese, Japanese, Southeast Asians, and many Polynesians).

Most of the differences among these people could be categorized as cultural differences. In many cases this would also refer to foreign national differences, but not always. The Native American culture differs greatly from the Latin-American culture of many urban areas and they are both quite different from non-minority group Caucasians—yet all three coexist in the United States.

While blacks and whites continue to fight in America over transracial adoption practices, comparatively little is said about the cross-cultural aspects of adoption. One reason may be that while some cross-cultural adoption takes place within the United States, most does not. Negative attitudes about cross-cultural adoption may be expressed more often by citizens of other nations than by Americans. As increased feelings of nationalism have grown in developing nations that are struggling to raise themselves above subsistence level, fear and resentment have increased at the prospect that a number of the nation's youngsters are losing touch forever with their native language, customs, and heritage. One adoptive mother of a Latin-American child tried to communicate her understanding and acceptance of these fears to a well-educated young Central American woman who was visiting the United States. The young woman's response surprised her:

> "You say you can understand these fears? Well, fine, but I cannot. Some of the people of my country and countries like mine may say such things, but what good are their words? Do they clothe a child, put shoes on his feet, and food in his stomach? Do these same people take in homeless children, hold them close to make them warm, and love them and dry their tears? No! They only talk. Let those, whatever their nationality, who will love and care for the children have them, and let us hear no more talk of nationalism. For like so many times in the past, they are only words, empty and dead once they are spoken and of no real help to any living child."

Foreign adoption is almost always cross-cultural adoption. Great care must be taken by agencies and prospective parents alike to make certain that the adopting parents do understand all the ramifications of adopting a child of another culture. A recent case in Maryland demonstrates that some agencies are not doing all they can or should in this area, or parents are not fully grasping what it means to adopt a child who is different from themselves. An 8-year-old child who was adopted as an infant from Korea was recently relinquished by her adoptive parents because they could not deal with her foreign appearance.

Just like those who adopt transracially, those who adopt cross-culturally must realize their son or daughter will always be of the same racial group and will one day look like adult members of the society from which they are adopted. A charming Oriental boy with almond eyes will be an adult Asian member of society just as a petite Latin baby girl will be an adult Latin woman someday. These are not cute little puppies and kittens to be taken home one day and booted out later when, having lost some of their cuddliness, they begin to cause a few problems. Adoption is a lifelong commitment. Adopting parents *must* realize they are expected by society (but much more importantly, *by that child*) to stand with the child through the rough times as well as through the good times.

Depending on the age of the child, he will not understand much of what has happened as he is uprooted from one world, placed on an airplane, and discharged hours later, for all he knows, onto another planet, so striking are all the dissimilarities between his old world and that of his new parents. Different children react as distinctly as different adults might to sudden changes. Some, like Tanya (see chapter 5) seem to able to adjust rather quickly to the change.

Another little girl, age 4, who came from India said nothing for days. Her adopting parents had sent her a *Life Book* (a miniature photo and information album showing pictures and descriptions of her new family, their neighbors, friends, and her new home). She came off the plane clutching the well-worn book tightly. Her new family had been told she knew English well, yet the child spoke not a word for three days. She simply sat and watched. But on the fourth day, when one of her siblings picked up her *Life Book*, her response was immediate. "That's mine!" The spell was broken and she began to make friends with her new brothers and sisters, and of course, her parents.

It is unfortunate that all foreign adopting parents do not have the opportunity to escort their children home. Those who visit their children's country quickly learn how different everything is and can better understand their child's adjustment difficulties. Lana spoke Spanish to her children (see chapter 5) to help them feel a bit more comfortable, but it is not a simple matter of language differences. All the senses are affected. For instance, everything smells different. Tropical lands often smell of local flowers, such as bougainvillaea (most famous for its use in the original Hawaiian leis), and just as likely of garbage in an open alley, exotic cooking aromas, or of live animals, dogs, chickens, pigs, burros, llamas, elephants, or camels, depending on the country. Orphanages are alive with the smells of children—diapers if they are used, milk, hot rice, and damp plaster.

Even the air feels different—heavier, more humid, and quite warm and comfortable. Buildings are constructed in an open-air style to let breezes pass freely, with no thought given to air-conditioning, heating, or window screens. Flies and mosquitoes come and go. The animals, mentioned above, wander in courtyards and open patios.

Children are scantily clad and usually barefoot. Whether they live with a family or in an orphanage, they are accustomed to sleeping in a room full of adults and other children, since few children who will be adopted have the luxury of a private room. Is it any wonder these same children nearly go into shock upon finding themselves in a large luxurious home (by their standards) that is closed tightly and has an "artificial climate" and carpets and drapes on all sides? They are aghast at all the paraphernalia that is piled upon them (coat, hat, mittens, boots, scarf, or snowsuit) to go outside into a most inhospitable climate known as winter. And how are they expected to sleep in a sterile separate room in such deafening quiet?

One adoptive mother who years later visited Korea found

mothers there carry their babies on their backs so that the children are accustomed to a great deal of motion. Then she understood why her baby daughter has experienced difficulty years earlier adjusting to the quiet subdued life of crib and playpen. Any American social worker can tell prospective parents what a profound effect a change of caretakers has on any child, even a newborn. Children adopted from other cultures and countries face an endless array of changes. It is no surprise many have initial adjustment problems. Even so, adopting parents can learn about the culture their child comes from and do all they can to ease this transition.

Life Books can be prepared and sent ahead for toddlers and older children. They should carry pictures of all the new family members and their names. Pictures of other siblings, cousins, neighbor children, and the family pets are very important, as these are the characters with whom children will most quickly identify. Keep the wording simple because no fluent English speakers may be nearby. Many foreign persons know or recognize a few words in English, however. An adoptive parent who is not traveling to escort the new child home can still learn a great deal about the child's country through carefully selected reading, by visiting with others who are natives of the country, or by talking with those who have visited there. While it may not be easy to find Colombian, Korean, or Indian natives in the local community, they do exist and can be found at many universities and through various cultural clubs and associations. Adopting parents can ask questions that pertain directly to child-rearing practices in the child's native country and hopefully find ways to ease the new child into their family and life in America.

Finally, there are those also in America who strongly object to removing children from their original societies. Critics of the Vietnamese Operation Baby Lift and similar rescue operations have greatly affected international policy as other situations have occurred since that 1975 program which brought hundreds of starving Vietnamese babies and children out of the war zone. Cambodian children, for instance, were not allowed to leave Southeast Asia a few years later when their lives were threatened by the Pol Pot regime. Those who managed to flee their own country did not always survive once they reached Thailand and other supposedly safe areas. They were not allowed to leave under United Nations policies and many more died even while United States citizens were ready and willing to bring them to a better life. Most adoptive parents of Vietnamese children will testify that they do not believe their own children would have survived if left in their native land.

Rosemary Taylor, a teacher, worked as a volunteer in Vietnam until the fall of Saigon in 1975. Today she works with children and families in the refugee camps of Thailand and Cambodia. In a report presented to social workers and adoption personnel, she made her position and that of many adoptive parents, crystal clear.

"A child without a family is a child deprived of the most elementary human right. A child has a birthright to grow up in an atmosphere of love and family concern. It has no birthright to protein-deficient diets, to forks or chopsticks, to a bellyful of parasites, to a childhood free of caresses and parental encouragement. It has no birthright to a particular shape of house nor to speaking a particular language. It has a birthright to parental love.... The nationality or the citizenship of a child is a meaningless concept to a child who is dead or subnormal from the deprivation of institutionalization. Can an orphanage ever meet the needs of any abandoned child? Should we not try to meet the needs of a greater majority of homeless children by increasing the number of intercountry adoptions?"

Independent Adoption. Independent adoption is to some extent the foreign version of a privately arranged adoption in that no adoption agency is involved in the placement of the child. Prospective parents who choose independent adoption must contact a local agency to conduct their homestudy. Once the homestudy is completed, they may use it and their other documents to adopt a child from a Colombian orphanage, through a private individual in India, or a lawyer or private person in El Salvador or Costa Rica, or any of the many other countries that allow independent adoption.

In the United States a few states have laws specifically forbidding independent adoption. Other states have laws that are unclear, so interpretation is left up to a particular judge or the current child welfare system administration. Prospective parents are susceptible many times to the same dangers as in private or privately arranged adoptions. Certain individuals may attempt to turn adoption into a major moneymaking endeavor. Prospective parents need to check foreign sources carefully. At first glance this may seem difficult, if not impossible. In this sort of situation, prospective parents can do themselves a great favor by contacting a large foreign adoptive parent organization.

A Utah couple who was having serious problems with an unscrupulous adoption contact in Latin America responded to a letter they read in a national adoption magazine. The letter had been written by another adoptive parent who had lived in the country from which the Utah couple hoped to adopt. Although the newfound friends lived over 1,000 miles apart, the former overseas residents were able to help the prospective parents straighten out their difficulties. A few

months later, when the same unethical individual attempted
to set up operations in the assisting couple's state, they were
aware of his past record and able to warn a small adoption
agency director who was considering working with this questionable adoption source. Taking time to check information
carefully with others involved in adoption can pay for itself
many times over in the long run.

Despite the risks involved, many parents feel independent
adoption is the best option for them. Independent personalities who are used to doing things on their own
probably feel most comfortable with independent adoption.
Other individuals who prefer a bit more organization or
regulation in their lives may well feel more comfortable
working with an established adoption agency. Some, like
Wayne and Lana (see chapter 5), have little choice in the
matter, since they wanted a child from a specific country
and could find no agency operating there at the time.
Others, like Louis and Doris, felt that an independent adoption would bring them a child faster than an agency adoption. They had met others who had adopted through the
source they used and while they recognized the risk involved, they felt confident that this was somehow meant to
be. They are now using the same adoption adviser to adopt
their second child.

There are also stories which do not have such a happy
ending. Before Michael and Janet (see chapter 5) adopted
Nicky from Korea, they attempted a Latin-American independent adoption. A private individual from New York was
the contact and a little 3-year-old boy eagerly awaited the arrival of his new parents at the orphanage he called home.
However, because certain documents were not properly
filed by the relinquishing mother, the foreign national court
would not grant permission for the child to leave the

country. The biological mother could not be found again so
that the boy, caught by a legal technicality, was not allowed
to leave. Whether the unsigned document entanglement
was the fault of the independent adoption contact or not is
unknown, but Michael and Janet were devastated emotionally for months over the loss of a little boy that they already felt was their own.

Most United States courts and child welfare systems that
are opposed to independent adoption are concerned that
there is no agency to provide post-placement services, i.e., to
serve as a safety net for the adopting family. In most independent placements, if the adoption disrupts the child becomes a ward of the state, and the state or country must find
a new home for him. (Foreign children are not returned to
their country of birth, since once they leave there simply are
no provisions for their possible return.) Public agencies can
find themselves drawn into an area they know little about—
foreign adoption.

Prospective parents who find themselves in a situation in
which local government officials are opposed to independent adoption need to discover the basis of the opposi-
tion. If it is caused by fears of who will provide for the child
in case of an adoption disruption, or other problems that
might arise before the adoption is finalized, there is a solution. A number of private agencies will make an agreement
with adopting parents to fill in the "safety net gap" for an
independent foreign adoption placement. The parents usually pay several hundred dollars to the agency, somewhat
like a bond or insurance policy. An agreement is signed
between the adopting parents and the agency. In the event
that the adoption is not completed, the private agency will
take responsibility for finding a new home for the child.
Once the adoption is finalized, the agency refunds the ma-

jority of the deposit to the new parents, keeping a portion to cover their expenses, paperwork, and staff time.

Lana and Wayne used this method when they brought Rodrigo into the country because their state would not allow independent adoption at that time. They contacted a private agency and paid $600 to the agency to act as their representative in case they would not be able to complete the adoption. When they sent a copy of their son's certified adoption decree to the agency several months later, the agency sent them a check for $400 as per their original agreement. In this way, all bases were covered. The local state officials were not responsible for the child, so they permitted the adoption to proceed. The parents and, most important, the child were protected should anything go wrong. And the private agency itself had funds paid in advance, if their services had been required. The adoption was completed on schedule with no further complications.

Many potential problems in adoption (whether foreign, domestic, transracial, cross-cultural, open, private, or independent) can be resolved if all parties remain calm and search for innovative and creative solutions to the problems as they arise. Unfortunately, emotions run high in adoption. Local politics and power plays can put extra pressure on all involved. Prospective parents must look for the answers when the red tape tangles. While they can expect assistance from agency personnel, government officials, and others, they need to be prepared to do it themselves, if necessary. There is a place for the old saying, "If you want it done right, do it yourself," in adoption. Prospective parents are building a family. They should not be afraid to take a firm confident hand in the project. After all, they know better than anyone else how they want the job done.

12

How will we know the right child for us?

The only question as difficult to answer might be the one that was in the minds of most prospective mothers and fathers a few years earlier, "How do I know this is the right man (or woman) for me?"

No one can give a prospective parent the right answer, yea or nay, but there are a number of things that when considered, might help to guide them.

Occasionally, the statement is made, "I'm afraid I wouldn't love an adopted child as much as my own [biological] child."

One adoptive father's answer to that comment was: "How can anyone say that and then look their wife (or husband) straight in the face? You are not biologically related to your spouse. You haven't known that person all your life. You don't know their entire past history, but you still love her (or him). So why do you have to be biologically related to your kids to love them?"

Many adoptive parents characterize meeting and learning

about their older children as similar to meeting, falling in love, and marrying. Such a commitment does not spring up overnight. Just as love at first sight is rare outside of romance novels, it is rare also between soon-to-be adoptive parents and their potential new children. And even if the parents think they feel that way toward their new child, it is unlikely the child will return the affection. These new parents are strangers to the child. He needs time, on his own or neutral turf, to come to know them before anything is expected of him.

When Lana (chapter 5) arrived in Central America to bring her new son home, he was unwilling to allow her to touch or hold him the first evening she arrived. That came as no surprise to her. But the next morning she woke up quite ill with a bad cold and cough and had to stay in bed for two days. She was afraid to get too close to Rodrigo for fear he would also get sick. He had time to watch her and approach her himself in his walker.

At first, Lana was disappointed with the turn of events. But after a few days, she realized it had a good side. She and her son had come to know each other slowly, according to his own timetable, not hers.

The old line, "Mom loved you best," is still a common joke in America regarding sibling rivalry. Ask any mother of more than one child and she will say, "You love each one differently because each one is different." Mothers love their sons in a different way than they love their daughters, and fathers love their daughters in a manner different from the way they love their sons. This does not make a parent's love for a son or daughter less strong or genuine than the love he has for the other. And so it is with the children a parent adopts. When one speaks to a remarried widow or widower they love the second spouse differently from the first. Not necessarily more or better, deeper or less fully, but just differently.

Some children are harder to raise than others. Some always seem to be going off in the wrong direction, out of step with others their age, while some are easier to raise and rarely seem to get out of line. This is not a limiting factor on whether parents love them or not. It is simply a fact of life. In a column entitled "My Favorite Child," Erma Bombeck noted that the child she loves the most is the one who needs her most at the moment. If such were the case for all, children in need of adoptive homes could be at the head of the line as everyone's favorite, for they are the ones who need parents the most.

Parents who are hoping to adopt a child would do well to remember the advice given to them as they were about to walk down the aisle: "Be prepared to accept him (or her) as he is. Don't marry him thinking you'll change him because you won't." When adopting, parents need to be able to accept a child as he or she is. While some behavior problems may be changed or modified over time with counseling, some will not. Prospective parents who take a child with the idea of totally changing or remaking the child are probably charting a course for disaster. One grandmother put it bluntly: "You can't beat out what's bred in." A foreign child, a child of another race, an older child, a mentally retarded child, or a physically handicapped child will still have these same characteristics as an adult, so parents must be certain of their expectations when they adopt.

In comparing adoption to marriage, it is sobering to ponder the current divorce rate in the United States of nearly 50 percent. What happens to adoptions that do not work out? Estimates vary considerably on how many adoptions end up in disruption, the equivalent of a divorce—depending on the area, the type of children, and the category of adoptive parents. The estimates for disruption in infant adoptions, foreign or domestic, are at less than 5 percent. But some estimates go as high as 20 percent for adoptions involving older, disturbed, or seriously troubled children. Since it is difficult to compile facts and figures on so many different types of adoption, it is also difficult to estimate how many disrupt.

The reasons for these breakups are as numerous as the reasons for divorce, but most fall under one large umbrella—unfulfilled expectations. This would include parents who have no real conception of what life with a child truly consists of; children who do not adjust to a family's lifestyle; parents who are divided over the adoption, and are therefore unable to commit themselves to the child; and, on occasion, a child who for one reason or another decides he does not want to be adopted. These are not pleasant situations but they must be faced and recognized as a part of the world of adoption. Hopefully, parents who are aware of the potential pitfalls can avoid them. Despite a high divorce rate, couples continue to marry in ever increasing numbers, and likewise, adoptions are on the rise.

Adoption can and does open up new horizons on family life that many otherwise would never have the opportunity to enjoy and experience. Like all human relationships, adoption carries the potential for both great joy and great pain. No one can give prospective parents any sort of a guarantee anymore than a pregnant woman gets any guarantees. Like birth, the action is caused by adults. Adopt is a verb. Children become "adopted," innocent victims shunted about, with the adults doing the adopting.

As adults, prospective parents must make the decision

when and if to adopt a particular child. There will be no lightning bolts from the sky with a brilliant glowing message, "This is *the* child." Many parents have traveled the road marked adoption before you. They trusted in God and their own abilities to be good parents. Guided by their faith and determination, they have made adoption one of the great loving experiences of human existence.

13

How much should we tell our adopted child?

(And what if she wants to search for her biological relatives?)

Legacy of an Adopted Child

Once there were two women
Who never knew each other.
One you do not remember;
The other you call mother.

Two different lives shaped
To make yours one.
One became your guiding star;
The other became your sun.

The first gave you life and
The second taught you to live in it.
The first gave you a need for love
And the second was there to give it.

One gave you a nationality;
The other gave you a name.
One gave you the seed of talent;
The other gave you an aim.

One gave you emotions;
The other calmed your fears.
One saw your first sweet smile;
The other dried your tears.

One gave you up—
It was all that she could do.
The other prayed for a child,
And God led her straight to you.

And now you ask me through your tears
The age-old questions through the years,
Heredity or environment—which are you the product of?
Neither, my darling, neither.
Just two different kinds of love.

—Anonymous

What to tell, what not to tell, and how to tell it. These are questions that have haunted adoptive parents since the day Pharaoh's daughter found baby Moses hidden in a basket in the reeds along the Nile (Exodus 2:1-10). As different methods of child care have come and gone, so also have various theories of what adopted children should and should not be told.

As children grow, they are naturally curious. An intrinsic part of childhood is discovering how things work, how things are constructed (and how they come apart), why certain things happen the way they do, and where everything comes from, and why. In years past, a great many children were never told they were adopted. Since most states seal the adoption file, including the original birth certificate, and issue a new birth certificate which states the child is the son or daughter of the adopting parents, it was not too difficult to cover such a ruse. A few adopted individuals never learned the truth. But most did, sooner or later. Because so much subterfuge had been employed and because the discovery was often accidental, from a slip of the tongue of a relative to the discovery of adoption forms amongst the deceased adoptive parents' private papers, the psychological trauma was often greatly accentuated.

While this may sound like the sticky plot of some daytime serial, it was all too often a real-life crisis for many individuals. Well intentioned but misinformed parents and caring relatives truly believed *not* telling a child or adult of their adoption would somehow protect them from all sorts of imagined emotional pains and assure the adoptive parents that their child would love only them. (It makes one thankful that much of the cloak-and-dagger era of adoption history is in the past.) Today, it is the highly unrealistic parent who does not tell their child when he or she has come into the family through adoption.

Many parents still find themselves uncomfortable with the topic, but fortunately this too is changing. Most social workers and experienced adoptive parents advise newly adoptive parents to begin early with adoption talk. Parents who adopt an infant or toddler can literally practice using the word "adoption" and telling their child how happy they are to have them as their very own son or daughter. By the time the child is old enough to understand a bit about the subject, the parents should feel more relaxed with the concept of adoption and the needed explanations.

Parents who adopt older children, especially those who have spent some time in foster care, will have a different set of circumstances to deal with. But they will still need to be certain the big word "adoption" is not just another piece of legal mumbo jumbo as far as their child is concerned. Children often pick up misconceptions regarding various human relationships (such as love, sex, and marriage) from others their age, and adoption is no exception. Adopting parents should work hard to help their children understand that this is a long-term binding relationship that includes many concepts including love, commitment, and security.

A 6-year-old boy picked up the mistaken idea that after a baby brother was born to his mother and father he would not be loved and wanted in the same way. A 4-year-old, who overheard her mother tell a friend she hoped to adopt two more children, tearfully asked her mother what family she and her brother would go to once the new children arrived. In such situations, children need to be instantly reassured.

Many parents will find they need to tell the particular child's adoption story many times over before their child will grasp all of its significance. A 3-year-old may simply be fascinated with the word, like one tiny dark-eyed beauty who kept repeating, "I'm Daddy's li'l 'dopted angel." A 4-year-old, on the other hand, asked his mother to tell him about his adoption again. When she finished, she assumed by his downcast expression that he had not understood much of what she had said, until he looked up and asked, "Why didn't she keep me?"

Sooner or later, most children come around to the matter of the biological mother's relinquishment. How they perceive this is a central issue of the entire adoption information question. Several approaches have commonly been used in attempting to explain the biological mother's reasons for relinquishment. They seem to fall into three categories—the good, the bad, and the impersonal.

 According to the good theories, adoptive parents tell their child that the biological mother let him go so that he could have a better life and to provide him with a real home and two loving parents. This explanation is used most often when the relinquishing mother is known or believed to be an unwed teenager or an undernourished poverty-stricken foreign mother. In both cases, the merit lies in the fact that no ill will is ever extended toward the child. Only good feelings and loving thoughts of the baby and his welfare are involved.

A few adoptive parents find this explanation implausible or objectionable because they feel it may confuse the child's perception of love. If the biological mother could give him away even though she loved him, what will it mean in terms of security when his adoptive parents say that they love him? This objection hinges on the belief that a child cannot grasp or understand more than one perception of love. One must also wonder if adoptive parents who object to telling a child that his first mother loved him feel threatened by the biological mother and her love for her child.

According to the bad theory, which no caring person ever uses as an explanation to an adopted child, the biological mother did not care for this child and that is why she gave him away. On rare occasion, such as with rape or incest, a biological mother may not care for her child, but this is highly unusual. The vast majority of women who carry a baby within their own body for nine months care deeply about him before and after he is born. Even in the case of an older adopted child, where abuse and neglect have been involved, biological parents usually care about their child. But they are so overwhelmed by their own problems or mental and emotional conditions that they are unable to transform those feelings into the normal loving actions between parent and child.

Perhaps such theories about "bad" biological mothers grew out of the need of social workers, adoptive parents, and others to justify the birth mother's actions and to make her somehow less threatening to the adoptive family. Certainly much of the secrecy that has surrounded adoption in the past grew out of misconceptions and misplaced fears held by all three parties—the adoptive parents, the agency, and the biological parent. Adoptive parents feared their children might love them less if they knew they were adopted. Adoptive parents and adoption agencies also feared society would ridicule the adopted child. But most of all biological parents feared it might be discovered they had relinquished a child for adoption.

One of the oldest myths in society is that only a bad, uncaring mother would give up her own baby. Good mothers keep their children no matter what. This is a ridiculous stereotype but, nonetheless, a widely believed one. Even now it continues to make life more difficult for relinquishing mothers. There is a thin line between unselfish relinquishment and self-indulgent disposal of a child, as far as much of society is concerned.

One of the saddest backlash effects of these bad theories is that the child will perceive himself as a part of the biological mother, as coming from her. And if she is bad, then he must be also. A child may feel guilty over his illegitimacy, that he comes from bad stock, or that he *did* something bad or naughty to make his first mother relinquish him. Bad theories are little more than a hodgepodge of the old fears, stereotypes, and myths that have swirled about the edges of the adoption issue for decades. All are false and can be dangerous to the child's mental and emotional well-being.

Finally, many professional social workers are currently promoting a relinquishment theory that makes no good or bad judgments about the mother or her child. Adoptive parents are encouraged to tell their son or daughter that his biological mother was too young (or sick or poor or confused) to take care of *any* baby, thereby depersonalizing the situation. This woman was not capable of raising any child, so she made a plan for someone else to care for and love the child. In this way, the adopted child can see that no personal rejection was involved and that he was not simply abandoned. Someone was in control of the situation at all times and making careful plans concerning his future. A parent might even ask a 6- or 7-year-old (or older) if he or she feels they could totally care for a baby at this time in their life. Since the answer will be "no" the parent can then continue by stating that the biological mother was also very young and unable to raise a child by herself.

Perhaps many of the intricacies of this side of the adoption question can best be understood by looking at adoption from the points of view of the social worker, the adoptive parent, the biological parent, and the adopted child. The feelings of all of these individuals are represented in the following account of Molly, who is both a social worker and an adoptive mother, and her family.

Molly lives on the outskirts of a major metropolitan area. During the 1960s and '70s, she worked with a total of 63 unmarried mothers, 38 of which made the difficult decision to relinquish their child. While this in no way involved any sort of scientific study, this group of young women (both black and white) included young mothers of all ages and economic levels, from an uneducated 15-year-old backwoods girl to a 35-year-old woman with a master's degree.

Molly talked with all of the mothers. She found their reasons for relinquishment, listed below, were remarkably similar despite the young mothers' other differences. (There has been no attempt to list these motives in order of priority of importance.)

(1) All of the relinquishing mothers felt they were not in a position to give their child a real home.

(2) All wanted two parents for their child.

(3) All wanted to further their own education and felt raising a child alone would be incompatible with their future educational endeavors.

(4) All wanted a better life for their child and felt their decision to relinquish was made out of love.

(5) All cried at the court hearing which terminated their parental rights.

(6) All 63 young women took several months to reach a decision on whether or not to relinquish their child.

Meanwhile, Molly and her husband, George, had adopted two infant sons, Gary and David, who are now teenagers. Molly's family, like many others, has always discussed adoption in an open and relaxed manner. She began telling both boys of their own adoptions at an early age. She used a magazine article she had found which showed a mother cat nursing several kittens and two "adopted" puppies whose mother was unable to nurse them. She explained that much like the mother cat had accepted two babies that were not originally hers, so she and their father had taken them, Gary and David, to love and raise as their very own. The interesting point has been the boys' very different reactions to their own adoptions. Molly attributes this, just as several major studies have done with adult adoptees, directly to their distinct personalities.

Gary, two years older than his brother, has never been very interested in adoption. He is a naturally easygoing type who accepts things as they come. Gary likes to take things apart and enjoys mechanics and figuring out how things work. However, he does not seem driven to explore the mysterious process that brought him to the couple he knows and loves as his mother and father.

David, on the other hand, has been fascinated with the subject. Ever since he was a preschooler he has asked an array of questions. His mother has done her best to answer each one in a way she felt was appropriate for his age. (Molly feels it is important for parents to evaluate their child's psychological need for the information and their ability to handle it at any specific age and level of development.) A glimpse of some private conversations between this adoptive mother and her son gives some insight into how a sensitive parent can handle some delicate questions with patience, love, and understanding.

> *David (age 4):* Is my first mother dead? I think she is.
>
> *Molly:* I really don't know, sweetheart. What makes you think so?
>
> *David:* I don't know. I just think she is. If she is, when I get big, will you take me to visit her grave?
>
> *Molly:* Well, I don't think she's dead, but if she is and you still want to visit her grave when you're grown, I'll take you.

(Molly thought of this conversation in retrospect and wondered if this was his way of "safely" introducing what he might have feared would be an upsetting subject to his mother. David has no recollection of this conversation and is amused when his mother speaks of it now.)

> *David* (age 5): I don't think my first mother is really dead. Do you think I could meet her someday when I grow up?
>
> *Molly:* When you grow up, if you still need to, yes.
>
> *David* (age 8, arguing in the backyard with a neighborhood playmate): I do so have two mothers! My mother told me I had another mother before her. Mom! Don't I have another mother?!
>
> *Molly:* Yes, you had a mother who gave birth to you. Now I'm the mother who loves you every day and in every way.
>
> *Neighbor Child's Mother* (ten minutes later in a frantic telephone call): Molly, how do I explain adoption to Mike! I don't know where to begin!

David (age 10): Mom, will you help me when I'm grown up to find my first mother?

Molly: Yes, I'll help you. I would also like to meet her. I'd like to tell her how much I appreciate her allowing you to grow up here with us. I want to tell her how much I have enjoyed life with you, loving and raising you. (Molly stops a moment to take a deep breath.) I want very much to thank her, but . . . we must remember that she has been very considerate of you and our family by allowing you to grow up here without contacting you or interfering in our life in any way. We must be equally respectful of her privacy and personal life and allow her to decide *if* she wants to be contacted by her biological child and his family. It must be her decision.

David (age 12): Did I have another name before you adopted me? Did my biological mother name me?

Molly freely admits that she hesitated momentarily on this question. She worried a bit about giving him this piece of information. But she decided if he was asking, he must need it, and she gave him the full name as she knew it. It has not caused problems as she initially feared. Quite the contrary, this new information has satisfied him for the time being. He has enjoyed "playing" with it mentally, trying it out, repeating it. Molly has from the beginning laid a solid foundation regarding David's desire to search for his biological mother. The key words "when you grow up" have been used time and again. While David knows his mother will help him when he is an adult, there is no doubt that in their family, a teenage search is out of the question.

As David grows older and the time draws nearer to when he might actually make a search, he seems to be growing calmer about the subject and a bit more introspective. Gary is still totally disinterested in the subject. After talking with

David one afternoon and answering more of his questions, Molly suggested to Gary that he too might want to search one day for his biological mother. His answer was definite. "Mom, I know my brother needs to find and meet his biological mother. I hope he gets to one day, since it is so important to him. But I really don't feel the need or desire to do so. If you want to meet her, you can find her. But I really don't want to."

Interestingly, Molly did inadvertently meet her eldest son's biological mother, Jane, a few years ago. It was not a planned or arranged meeting but came about through a coincidental sequence of events too long to record here. No search was conducted by either woman. Both Molly and Jane were shocked to find themselves face to face. However, after each had taken a few moments to regain her composure, they decided to take advantage of the opportunity to exchange information.

Molly thought Jane's first breathless questions were significant of her true feelings. "Is he alive? healthy? happy? well adjusted?" After hearing a definite "yes" to each question, she took a deep breath and seemed to relax. "Thank God! I have *willed* him to be happy and have prayed for him all these years, but it is still good to actually hear it for myself." She was also glad to learn that her son was still in school, was a good student, had a job, and was being raised in the church Jane had requested when she relinquished him. Jane said she had been afraid that as an adopted child everything might have been handed to him. Molly was happy to lay another adoption myth to rest as she assured Jane that such was not the case.

Molly also had questions that revolved around the biological family's physical and emotional characteristics, such as height, hair color, and the love of a challenge. Jane and

Molly had agreed as their conversation began that they would both say "no" to any question that made them uncomfortable. Jane asked Molly's last name and where she lived, but Molly did not feel ready to divulge that information and Jane said she understood.

As their conversation neared an end, Jane told Molly she had no intention of interfering and that she had no need to meet Gary now that she knew he was all right. She invited Molly to contact her anytime she cared to, since her husband knew she had relinquished a baby for adoption as a teenager. As Molly was preparing to leave, Jane commented that she was surprised that Molly had not asked why she had given up her child. Molly touched her hand lightly as she said, "I assumed it was out of love."

Jane answered with tears in her eyes, "You are the first person to ever say that to me." She explained that she was from a family who had raised their children on welfare and she had not wanted the same for her son. He had been conceived in what she thought was love, but the father of the child had not returned her affection. So as an unwed 16-year-old, she had relinquished the baby. Shortly afterward she enrolled in a government training program and had worked hard to reach her current position as a hospital nurse. As Molly left, Jane told her, "Continue raising your son and thank you for doing such a beautiful job."

Molly says Gary still has no interest in finding his biological relatives. She has, however, recorded the information she discovered so that he will have access to it if he ever changes his mind. The search of many adult adoptees for their biological roots is triggered by a crisis such as the death of the adoptive parents, a divorce, or a life-threatening experience. A search may also be inspired by life's momentous occasions, including marriage and the birth of a child.

Elizabeth Scott is a regional director with the American Adoption Congress, an umbrella coalition group of over 300 separate adoptee and birth parent organizations across the United States and Canada. She has been successful in 97 percent of the searches in which she has assisted. She has helped in a few searches involving a minor but only when he or she was accompanied by one of the adoptive parents. Her advice for those who wish to search is that they contact a reputable search consultant. "Many adult adoptees and birth parents originally contact a lawyer and pay a large fee, often for nothing," she points out. "Lawyers and other individuals who are not experienced in searching rarely help their clients. Just as prospective parents can lose money to unreliable adoption sources, biological relatives who are trying to locate each other can lose money to unscrupulous types who collect on their emotional turmoil." Ms. Scott suggests those who are interested in searching, contact the American Adoption Congress (P.O. Box 44040, L'Enfant Plaza Station, Washington, D.C. 20026-0040), which can connect them to legitimate search consultants in their immediate area.

As a search consultant, Ms. Scott has helped in over 200 different searches and she works in conjunction with a licensed social worker. She often serves as the third party who makes the initial contact with the biological relative. "No one should just turn up on someone else's doorstep," she cautions. "Birth mothers and fathers and adult adoptees all deserve more privacy and consideration than that. The idea is to approach people gently and thoughtfully."

In all her cases, Ms. Scott has come across only one biological mother who adamantly refused to see her 21-year-old son. In one other case, she found an unusual situation. She located the birth mother a young woman was searching for.

While the older woman was not opposed to meeting her daughter, it was revealed that the mother was a highly paid escort and had given up a number of babies for adoption.

In all other instances, Scott has found both the adoptee and the biological parent(s) to be average hard-working people. The mothers generally found themselves to be in a situation they simply could not handle and had chosen adoption as the best alternative for their child.

Elizabeth Scott herself is an adult adoptee whose adoptive father aided her in her search for her biological mother. Today she knows several half brothers and sisters as well as a biological brother. She found them all and feels her own searches have greatly enriched her life. They have also deepened the relationship between herself and her father, not harmed it, as many have been led to believe in the past. "I realize now that my brothers and sisters have had a more difficult life and certainly have more adjustment problems right now than I do," she says. "It's not too hard to figure out who is responsible for me having a better chance in life than they did." Today, because of her own experiences, Elizabeth Scott can sympathize and empathize with her many searching clients.

Some adoptive parents view the very idea of their adopted child searching for other relatives as an affront, some sort of threat, or personal failure. Molly has heard more than one adoptive parent comment, "But my children never asked about adoption."

Molly's answer is quick and to the point. "That's simple. Children learn at an early age that some questions are simply not to be asked and are not allowed in their household. They can sense unspoken attitudes and see that when the subject is mentioned, the parent is very uncomfortable or even hostile. They quickly learn not to ask again."

Adoptive parents need to be more relaxed with the idea of adoption searches. Estimates from European countries with open adoption records for many years show that only about 10 percent of all adopted individuals ever search for the biological relatives. The average searcher is in his or her mid to late twenties. While many teens may bring up the subject to test the waters, most do not follow through in later years. The teenage years are such a tumultuous time for all persons. An occasional adopted teen can become confused about the cause of his or her extra-emotional feelings. It is easier to blame adoption for the emotional upheaval in their life than to accept it as a natural, normal part of development. Likewise, most teens do not need any extra emotional baggage, such as a relative search, until their feet are a bit more securely planted.

Nora, age 29, searched for genealogical information on her biological parents whom she believed to be dead. Instead she found both her parents alive in a rural mountainous area. Her parents were poor uneducated hill people. When her father had decided for some reason that Nora was not his biological child, her mother had put the baby up for adoption, apparently out of fear for her daughter's safety. An only child, Nora also found she had a houseful of biological siblings. She found her brothers and sisters viewed her with a certain amount of envy, feeling she was the lucky one who had "gotten out." She had been raised by middle-class parents and had a college education. Her brothers and sisters had not had such advantages or opportunities.

Nora conducted her search for information without telling her adoptive mother. When it came time for her to confide in her mother, she found it quite difficult. She was certain the truth would hurt her widowed mother. Her mother, however, became very concerned. She sensed that her daughter wanted to share some sort of dire news. So when Nora finally blurted out her story, her mother merely blinked in surprise and let out a huge sigh of relief. "Is that all? I was afraid you had some terrible disease or that you had lost your job or something really serious like that!"

Adoptive parents need to realize that a child's interest in his biological family is not a threat or an insult. Some individuals are simply more naturally curious than others. Many parents love more than one child, so it should not come as any great shock that their children can care for more than one parental figure. Adoptive parents should also remember that while biological relatives may visit and answer each other's questions, most do not form close relationships. Like Nora, they have little in common. Many feel as Nora stated later, "I'm glad I found my biological family. It answered some of my questions. But searching was never something that took over my life. I did not let it interfere with my job, my family, my responsibilities, and the rest of my life." Of the new close relationships that do form, they are usually friendships, not parent-child relationships. The time for that is long past.

Adoptees also need to remember that their adoptive parents' objections to searching may be based on old stereotypes and fears of losing their child's affections. Equally strong can be the fear that their child will discover some awful and painful fact about their biological parents, themselves, or the circumstances of the adoption. Just as a parent runs to catch a falling toddler, parents of adult children instinctively try to protect them from life's emotional hurts and jolts. While Elizabeth Scott's experiences show that only a tiny percentage of adoptees are likely to uncover dark secrets, it is still a common fear.

However adoptive parents decide to handle the information they know and the questions their child asks, experienced adoptive parents, adult adoptees, and social workers agree that children should be told about their adoption beginning the day they arrive in their new home. Above all, parents should not lie or tell fairy tales of any sort. The old Mummy-and-Daddy-picked-you-out-of-*all*-the-others story may cause children to believe they were selected at a baby supermarket where parents can squeeze, pinch, shake, and check out the lot before choosing the one that is "just right."

When the day of disillusionment comes (and it most certainly will for those who are given such fanciful accounts of their adoption), it can lead a child to wonder, "And what else didn't they tell me the truth about?" Children's imaginations are active enough without parents further smudging the lines between fantasy and reality. Most children are tougher and smarter than their parents give them credit for being, no matter what their age. Most can handle the truth, even if it is a simple "I don't really know," as long as it is presented in a loving understanding manner.

A few biological mothers know the value of telling the child the truth, even though the child may still be only an infant. Molly had the privilege to listen to one 16-year-old as she held and kissed her baby good-bye. The young mother said, "I know you are very new to this world, but I want you to listen to me. Never forget this day. I love you very much. Because I love you, I want you to have the very best this world has to offer. I can't give it to you. I wish I could, but I just can't right now. I want you to have two parents, a good home, security, and most of all, lots and lots of love. There's a social worker here. Her name is Molly. She says she can find you a home and a family with all those things, so I am going to give you to her. I don't want you to forget. I love you. I will always love you. I will pray every day for you and your new parents. I will never ever forget you."

It's been nearly 20 years since Molly sat in that particular hospital room. She still cannot speak of that young mother with dry eyes. When she hears rude comments made about birth mothers and their lack of love, she remembers. She knows better.

14
Open records—should we or shouldn't we?

*I*n Indiana a wealthy biological aunt of a child relinquished for adoption years before left $250,000 to her nephew in her will. The adoption agency refused to let the money be passed on to the child. They cited closed records policies and said that the child in question was no longer a legal relative of the deceased woman (not a requirement to receive a bequest from a deceased person's estate). The adoptive family was never informed or consulted.

•In Michigan a mother who had given up a child for adoption returned to the agency several years later because a child born to her later in life was suffering from a neuromuscular disease. She felt the adoptive family of her first child should know, but the agency refused to pass the information along since she could not prove beyond any doubt that the disease was hereditary. The agency did not want to risk upsetting the adoptive family. Yet if their decision was wrong; the adopted child will be kept in jeopardy without the knowledge of his parents.

•In Missouri, in a well-publicized court case, a Florida resident has been seeking to open his adoption records because he is dying of leukemia. His only hope is a bone marrow transplant from a close blood relative, either a parent or sibling. This father of two young children has been denied access to the adoption file in question. The law in this case is open to interpretation by the judge. It states that records may be opened only when a *compelling need* is present. A Kansas City judge has ruled against the man in this case, stating that he does not meet the requirements as defined by law. If dying is not compelling need, what is?

As more states consider legislation allowing adult adoptees, birth parents, and the adoptive parents to see their respective adoption records, the matter of open records has become a hotly contested issue. While it is not of immediate concern to most prospective adoptive parents, it is something they and the rest of the country will continue to hear about for a long time. Those whose lives are touched by adoption will have to deal with it personally in the future one way or another.

What makes the open records issue such a controversial one is the three large groups of individuals involved—adult adoptees, adoptive parents, and birth parents—and the fact that many from each group are found on both sides of the fence.

Many adult adoptees object to closed adoption records strictly on principle. All law-abiding citizens over the age of 21 are theoretically entitled to see government, employment, and other files on themselves which contain personal and private information. A judge, a court clerk, or a social worker may look at an adult adoptee's file which lists his biological mother's name and most times the biological father's name and a few other details concerning the adoptee's birth, relinquishment, and adoptive placement. Even so, the adult adoptee is barred from examining this same file. In other words, the law regards the adoptee forever as a child, a person of minor involvement in the case, no matter what his or her age and despite the fact that the whole process revolves around the adoptee and his or her welfare.

Understandably, adoptees resent the Godlike decisions being made about their lives by these same individuals such as the cases in Indiana, Michigan, and Missouri mentioned above. It is a bizarre situation. Under no other circumstances are noncriminals treated with so little regard for their personal freedom and decisions concerning their own lives. In one case, a child died of a rare hereditary disease partly because of the fact that the family and their doctor encountered great difficulty diagnosing the child's illness. The child's mother had relinquished a baby years earlier for adoption. After her child's funeral, she learned the adoption agency had been informed several years before that the adopted child was also suffering from the same disease. The information had never been passed on to the biological mother, however. The adopted child's family had access to excellent medical care and that child's survival rested greatly on early diagnosis and treatment of his condition. The biological mother bitterly denounced the agency's decision and the statutes that supported it, since early diagnosis might have also saved her child.

It is this critical area of little or no medical information passed on to the adoptive parents or back to the biological parents that poses the greatest risk to adoptees and their descendants. And this is probably the most forceful reason to open adoption records. While lack of information can be an annoyance when filling out forms in a doctor's office or when applying for a job or in dealing with minor allergic reactions, it can become life-threatening when certain cancers, organ malfunctions, or hereditary diseases are involved.

Whether or not adoptees are interested in searching for their biological relatives, are satisfied with their lives and are busy concentrating on the future instead of concerning themselves with the past, the rights of those who want to see their records and/or search can no longer be ignored.

Adoptive families have been told a number of things over the years regarding open adoption records. Most have accepted what they have been told, including the fact that closed records were instituted in the 1930s and '40s by trained professionals whose only interest was to protect the adopted child and his new family. No one seems to be clear on *what* or *whom* these individuals and families are being protected *from* and this is a matter which needs more scrutiny. Is it the "terrible truth" of the old myths and wives' tales, the disruptive influence of a birth parent, or the fear that the child will love a stranger more than his adoptive parents who have loved and guided him all of his life? All seem unlikely prospects. As was noted earlier, few adoptees discover any terrible truths locked in those secret adoption files or in their searches for biological relatives.

Despite television dramas and rumors to the contrary, most adoptees are no more likely to discover any great skeletons in the closet than they are to discover that their biological mother is a movie star or their biological father is a millionaire oil baron. They rarely discover anything more dramatic than an unwed birth mother who felt unprepared to raise a child alone. Biological mothers are not out to cause problems in their children's lives (see chapter 13). As one biological mother quietly remarked at a meeting of adult adoptees and birth parents: "I would never search for my son. He was a beautiful baby and he will be 24 very soon. I'd love it if he would search for me and I'd be happy to see him, but I wouldn't risk disrupting his life by looking for him."

Some adult adoptees who wish to look at their adoption records do not do so to seek out a stranger to love. They know where "home" is and who raised, loved, and cherished them to help shape them into the persons they are today. Others, particularly if their adopted relationship is strained, may harbor hopes that a more satisfying family tie might be found in their biological roots. Adoptive parents who fear their child will love some new person more than he loves them need to closely examine their fears and their relationship with their child. Parents should recognize that both environmental and hereditary factors combine to form a whole person.

Taken one step further, the adoptive parents who are proud of their child should be pleased with their success in raising a fine young adult. They should also realize that many of the good traits and characteristics they love and admire came from two individuals known as his biological parents. Are they really likely to be unworthy persons if, together, they could produce such a beloved offspring? Many families adopt more than one child. If the parents can love more than one child without hurting or slighting the other(s), is it so difficult to concede that the child might love more than one parental relative, without hurting or neglecting either?

But the open records battle continues. Myths and old stories are perpetuated that play upon the emotions and uncertainties of adoptive families and biological mothers. For instance, some birth mothers do not tell their husbands and children that they gave up a child for adoption years earlier.

Some feel certain their current families would never understand. While it is true that such a discovery years later can
create havoc in a biological mother's life, the situation is to a
certain extent of her own making since she made the decision whether or not to tell her spouse.

Most adult adoptees use a third party contact or contact
the birth parent quietly and discreetly. Most, like Jane
(chapter 13), will undoubtedly need some time to regain
their composure, but several reunions have taken place
quietly without the birth mother's family's knowledge if that
is how she wants the matter handled. Biological mothers
who rely on the closed records system for protection are
playing a fool's game. Ninety-five percent of those who do
search with the help of a professional consultant find the
relatives they seek without the benefit of open records.
Closed records only make the search more difficult, more
prolonged, and more expensive, but they do not stop, deter,
or prevent most determined searchers from reaching their
goal.

Meanwhile, old arguments (such as the one that infant relinquishments will plummet to near zero if birth mothers'
identities are not protected) wear thin. Relinquishments
from states like Kansas, which has had open records since
1951, show no marked decreases or increases, regardless of
the open or closed status of the adoption records.

Much more disturbing are those who fight vehemently
against open records even though they themselves are not
adoptees, adoptive parents, nor birth parents. Some of these
have been involved in the past with the placement of
children, especially infants. In a number of cases children
were placed illegally through black market connections, or
with parents who were never approved by any agency for
one reason or another. A number of homes for unwed

mothers were involved in both the legal and the illegal baby business.

In some cases, relinquishing mothers were told their babies were stillborn when, in fact, they were not. Once a mother believed her baby was dead, there were, of course, no relinquishment documents to be signed. Meanwhile, the baby was placed for adoption however the home or the individual in charge saw fit. This sort of deceit and conspiracy has come to light in an occasional case as searchers have overcome the legal obstacles in their path. Many professional searchers believe nationwide open records would reveal a great deal more of this sort of activity. Since many of the individuals involved are still living, they want to make certain all adoption records remain sealed.

One thing is clear. There are still many misconceptions and unfounded fears and rumors floating in the murky waters that surround the open records matter. The original secret adoption system that was established 50 years ago does its best to imitate the birth process. It actually seems to be based on the old saw, "What you don't know won't hurt you." The adoption file which includes the original birth certificate is sealed and a new birth certificate listing the adoptive parents is issued. This follows the natural order of things, as perceived by the founders of the system, by trying to make the child adopted into the family resemble as much as possible the child who is born into the family.

Today social work professionals and adoptive families know it is wrong to totally equate the two. Adoption and birth are not the same. They are two different methods of entering a family and neither is superior to the other. Both are Celebrations of Life and Love. The greater emphasis should be on the love that grows once a child is part of the family, rather than on how, when, or at what age he arrived.

Those adoptees who wish to see their adoption files may do so in some states such as Hawaii, Alaska, Minnesota, and Pennsylvania which are beginning to follow Kansas' lead. A number of other countries (including England, Scotland, Wales, Finland, and Norway) also have open records and report no serious problems associated with the issue. (In many cases, however, adult adoptees may secure little more than their mother's maiden name which may well be a 30-year-old piece of information.)

Several adoption agencies have changed their policies in recent years. Those interested in open records/searching should recontact the adoption agency that was used, if possible. The agency may share the information they have on file or attempt to contact the biological relative concerned.

Slowly but surely, government employees, adoption agency personnel, and state legislators are beginning to recognize that a small but very vital portion of the population—adult adoptees—has been treated unjustly. The change is coming, if slowly. As one Maryland judge observed, "The adoption triangle needs to be an equilateral one with the interests and desires of all three sides given equal consideration. None of the three should dictate to the others."

In the years ahead, open records will become a reality. It is a matter of time and equal rights for all.

15
What if we need more help later?

*A*n adoptive couple with several children, both biological and adopted, was particularly concerned about their teenage son and his problems and took him to see a professional therapist. While the mother was interested in *family* counseling, this particular counselor seemed interested in seeing only the child in question. After a few therapy sessions, the counselor recommended that the adoptive parents return their adolescent son to the adoption agency because he "had too many problems"!

All families, both those formed by adoption and those formed by birth, on occasion have problems that require outside assistance. But because much of society, including some members of the professional community, still holds uninformed and negative opinions about adoption, adoptive families must use extra caution when seeking help.

The above situation could have resulted in unnecessary tragedy for the entire family, and especially for the young man at the center of the controversy. Fortunately, this family was not easily misled. As experienced adoptive parents, they recognized an unprofessional attitude and unreliable advice when they encountered it. They immediately sought out a different therapist, and this time the adoptive parents met with the counselor *first*. They asked a number of questions and also made their position clear. They let the counselor know from the beginning that they were a family that intended to stay together. They wanted counseling *as a family,* in addition to any individual therapy that their son or any other family member might require. The counseling sessions progressed much more smoothly the second time around.

Adoptive families must have a strongly defined position and a positive attitude from the outset. Professional therapists, like others, may have misconceptions about adoption. This family's first contact assumed adoption was not a permanent condition. It is highly unlikely that he would have so blithely suggested that a family "return" or "get rid of" their biological child. Adoptive families should not hesitate to let therapists, doctors, and others know that their commitment to their child is every bit as strong as that of a parent to a biological child. They will seek solutions as an indivisible family unit to any problems they face.

When problems of any sort develop in an adoptive family, one of the first decisions facing the family is to determine, if possible, whether the particular problem is related to the adoption and/or the child's past life. Four-year-old Wade (see chapter 1), for instance, decided he "caught" diabetes as a result of his adoption. His parents, of course, knew this was not true. But they had to explain the facts to Wade a number of times before they were able to convince him.

The circumstances may not be so clear-cut in the case of older children, including both those whose adoptions are relatively recent and those whose adoptions took place many years before. When teens and preteens begin to have serious problems at school, drink, use drugs, or fall into other confused and troubled behavior, their families are faced with attempting to determine the cause of the problem and whether it relates to the child's adoption. Other teenage actions and reactions—including moodiness, giddiness, withdrawn or argumentative behavior—may well be the result of one stage or another of adolescence. To help determine which problems are of real concern and which are more likely to be the result of normal teenage mood swings, adoptive families have a number of options available.

Depending upon their personal situation, adoptive families may want to recontact their adoption agency. Many agencies also offer family counseling programs in addition to their adoption services or are familiar with others who do. A counselor recommended or employed by an adoption agency will more likely appreciate the particular problems faced by adoptive families. Adoptive families must make certain, however, that by recontacting the agency they are *not* inadvertently sending a message to their child that says "we are considering returning you to where we found you." Rather, they should reassure their child that the family *as a unit* is returning to a source that has helped them in the past. Now that they have reached a point where they once again feel a need for outside assistance, they are going back to a resource they feel they can trust to help them again.

Of course, some families may not be able to turn to their original agency. They may have moved across the country or completed a non-agency adoptive placement or the adoption agency may no longer be in existence. Adoptive families may also contact their local public service agency, whether or not their child was placed by that same agency. Many public service agencies keep a list of professional counselors on file for use by their clients and others who may need family counseling at some point.

Adoptive families can also contact their local adoptive parents support group to determine if they know of any trained professionals who will help adoptive families. Some groups may not list such counselors. But usually a few member families, who have also sought help with their own families, may be able to recommend certain individuals. Perhaps, just as important, they may recommend which ones not to see. These families frequently know not only which professionals truly understand and appreciate the unique qualities of adoptive and foster families, but which make a real effort to keep their fees within the range of the average family budget.

Adoptive parents may also wish to contact family counselors and therapists directly through a local family center or the mental health association in their community. (Scanning the telephone directory is not a recommended method for finding any sort of doctor or therapist.) Parents need to be certain, however they find their particular counselor, that he or she understands the commitment involved in adoption. Persons seeking help should also remember that professional counselors and therapists, like all human beings, are fallible. When the advice of one seems totally contrary to a family's ideals and standards, they should not hesitate to seek another opinion.

In Marty and Marilyn's case (see chapter 1), their adoptive parents sought family counseling at a large military medical facility. Upon discovering evidence of Marilyn's brain damage, the military doctor in charge of the pediatric department seized custody of the two children and placed them in the hospital for 48 hours of observation. He did not have immediate access to the children's state medical records, documenting Marilyn's abuse history. Sid and Sarah were shocked and furious but it was not until the state produced the children's medical files and finally threatened to file suit, that the doctor involved admitted his mistake and released the children. Rather than checking the facts thoroughly beforehand, he assumed the adopting parents were the ones who had abused the children.

Despite such occurrences, adoptive families should never hesitate to seek help when they feel it might be needed. They should not delay for fear their family will not be immediately understood. When serious conditions or problems are involved, the risks can be too great.

Anita (chapter 3) felt momentary panic as she prepared to take Wade to the hospital when she realized he was not well. "I knew something was terribly wrong," she recalls. "He seemed so weak. He nearly fell down when I put his winter coat on him. I knew we needed help but a little hysterical voice kept screaming inside me, 'What if they think we somehow caused whatever is wrong with Wade? What if they try to take him away from us now, saying we are responsible for his weakened condition?' I knew it was ridiculous but it still scared me. When they discovered he had diabetes, I knew Otis and I would not be blamed, but then I was *really* scared we'd lose him in an even worse way if they could not control his illness."

If Anita and Otis had hesitated in seeking assistance, the end result could have been disastrous for their son. Today his diabetes is under control and Wade is growing and developing into a handsome young man.

There are many sources of assistance for families with children who have special needs. In addition to those listed in chapters 7 and 13, the following organizations can help families in need. Since most on this list are nonprofit organizations, please enclose a self-addressed stamped envelope when requesting information and assistance.

National Society for Autistic Children
1234 Massachusetts Ave. N.W.
Suite 1017
Washington, D.C. 20005

United Cerebral Palsy Assoc.
66 East 34th Street, 3rd Floor
New York, New York 10016

National Association for the Deaf-Blind
2703 Forest Oak Circle
Norman, Oklahoma 73071

Centers and Services for the Deaf-Blind Children
Room 3151, Donahue Building
400 6th Street S.W.
Washington, D.C. 20202

Mental Health Association, National Headquarters
1800 North Kent Street
Arlington, Virginia 22209

Epilepsy Foundation of America
4351 Garden City Drive
Landover, Maryland 20795

American Cancer Society
777 Third Avenue
New York, New York 10017

American Cleft Palate Assoc.
331 Salk Hall
Pittsburgh, Pennsylvania 15261

American Heart Association
7320 Greenville Avenue
Dallas, Texas 75231

American Lung Association
1740 Broadway
New York, New York 10019

Asthma and Allergy Foundation of America
19 West 44th Street, Suite 702
New York, New York 10036

The Candlelighters Foundation
2025 Eye Street, Suite 1011
Washington, D.C. 20006

Cystic Fibrosis Foundation
6000 Executive Blvd., Suite 309
Rockville, Maryland 20852

Juvenile Diabetes Foundation
23 East 26th Street, 4th Floor
New York, New York 10010

Leukemia Society of America
800 Second Avenue
New York, New York 10017

National Assoc. for Sickle Cell Disease, Inc.
3460 Wilshire, Suite 1012
Los Angeles, California 90010

National Hemophilia Foundation
19 West 34th Street, Room 1204
New York, New York 10001

National Kidney Foundation
Two Park Avenue
New York, New York 10016

National Tay-Sachs Foundation and Allied
    Diseases Association
122 East 42nd Street
New York, New York 10017

Alexander Graham Bell Association for the Deaf
3417 Volta Place N.W.
Washington, D.C. 20007

International Assoc. of Parents of the Deaf
814 Thayer Avenue
Silver Spring, Maryland 20910

International Parents Organization (Hearing Impairments)
3417 Volta Place N.W.
Washington, D.C. 20007

John Tracy Clinic (Hearing Impairments)
806 West Adams Blvd.
Los Angeles, California 90007

National Assoc. of the Deaf
814 Thayer Avenue
Silver Spring, Maryland 20910

Assoc. for Children and Adults with Learning Disabilities
4156 Library Road
Pittsburgh, Pennsylvania 15234

The Orton Society, Inc. (Learning Disabilities)
8415 Bellona Lane, Suite 115
Towson, Maryland 21204

Association for Retarded Citizens
2501 Avenue J, P.O. Box 6109
Arlington, Texas 76011

Down's Syndrome Congress
1640 W. Roosevelt Road
Room 156E
Chicago, Illinois 60608

American Brittle Bone Society
1256 Merrill Drive
West Chester, Pennsylvania 19380

Arthritis Foundation
3400 Peachtree Road N.E.
Suite 1106
Atlanta, Georgia 30326

Human Growth Foundation (Physically Handicapped)
4930 West 77th Street
Minneapolis, Minnesota   55435

Little People of America
P.O. Box 126
Owatonna, Minnesota 55060

Muscular Dystrophy Association
810 Seventh Avenue
New York, New York 10019

The National Assoc. of the Physically Handicapped, Inc.
76 Elm Street
London, Ohio 43140

Osteogenesis Imperfecta Foundation
632 Center Street
Van Wert, Ohio 45891

Spina Bifida Association of America
343 S. Dearborn Street, Room 319
Chicago, Illinois 60604

American Speech, Language, and Hearing Association
10801 Rockville Pike
Rockville, Maryland 20852

American Council of the Blind
1211 Connecticut Avenue N.W.
Suite 506
Washington, D.C. 20036

American Council of the Blind Parents
Rt. A, Box 78
Franklin, Louisiana 70538

American Foundation for the Blind
15 West 16th Street
New York, New York 10011

International Institute for Visually Impaired 0-7 Inc.
1975 Rutgers Circle
East Lansing, Michigan 48823

National Association for Parents of Visually Impaired
2011 Hardy Circle
Austin, Texas 78757

National Association for Visually Handicapped
305 East 24th Street
New York, New York 10010

National Federation of the Blind
1800 Johnson Street
Baltimore, Maryland 21230

March of Dimes Birth Defects Foundation
1275 Mamaroneck Avenue
White Plains, New York 10605

National Easter Seal Society for Crippled Children and Adults
2023 W. Ogden Avenue
Chicago, Illinois 60612

National Genetic Foundation
555 West 57th Street
New York, New York 10019

The Association for the Severely Handicapped
7010 Roosevelt Way, N.E.
Seattle, Washington 98115

The above list of organizations comes from CLOSER
LOOK, the national information center for handicapped
persons which was established to help parents of youth and
children by giving practical advice on how to find educational programs and other kinds of services. Parents and

others seeking assistance with problems and the needs of a mentally, physically, or emotionally disabled child or young adult can write directly to: CLOSER LOOK, P.O. Box 1492, Washington, D.C. 20013.

To obtain the appropriate type of information needed for a particular child, parents should be as specific as possible about the child's handicapping condition, whether known or suspected, the child's age, and the type of aid sought. The staff of CLOSER LOOK will respond with an appropriate packet of pamphlets, suggestions on steps to take to locate services, and other useful information.

In addition to these national organizations (and this list is not complete; there are many others), each state has a Crippled Children's Association. These organizations serve children with a wide variety of mental, emotional, and physical handicapping conditions. They can usually help parents locate specific services locally, aid in financial planning, and may even pay for a portion of the medical assistance that is needed. Parents can find the crippled children's services organization in their state by contacting their public health department.

In addition to these more serious problems experienced by relatively few adoptive families, all adoptive families are concerned about how their family and their children will be received and perceived by society in general. Many an adoptive family or child has found themselves under extra pressure to be constantly exemplary. This is, of course, impossible. It can even be detrimental to a child and his self-image and can produce emotional problems. Adoptive parents also need to discuss the negative and confusing messages they and their children will inevitably encounter in today's society from time to time. For example:

•A large metropolitan animal shelter encourages city

residents to adopt a cat or dog during a Be Kind to Animals Campaign. Such advertisements are often offensive to adoptive families since they may give children a number of false impressions about adoption. They may convey the idea that adopted children are picked out by their parents at some sort of shelter. Or worse, they may imply that, like a house pet, children might be returned if their behavior is unacceptable or if the family moves to an area where keeping them would be inconvenient.

•A small-town newspaper headlines the severe beating an older man received at the hands of his adopted son. There is no proof that the fact that the boy was adopted had any bearing on the case. This sort of publicity is especially damaging since the boy involved was a minor. The newspaper knew nothing about the personal life of this family and is simply perpetuating an unsubstantiated negative image of adoption.

•A number of toy manufacturers offer dolls for adoption, instead of for sale. This sort of advertising may send a confusing message to adopted children, including the idea that they might have been purchased or picked out of a store display window, or that adoption is not a permanent enduring lifelong relationship. These are not the sort of sentiments adoptive parents wish to convey to their children.

Most painful of all are individuals who ask intrusive or insulting questions in an insensitive manner. "Is he your own or adopted?" "Do you know who his real parents are?" "Isn't it a shame you can't have your own natural children?" "Isn't she lucky to have been adopted by you?" and so on. It takes a calm self-confident adoptive parent to answer such remarks in a smooth unruffled manner. The situation is even more painful when the child who is old enough to understand the slight is within earshot.

Probably no two words cause more resentment among adoptive families than the words *real* and *natural*. If biological parents or birth children are real or natural, does that make adoptive parents or adopted children unreal or unnatural? In a polite but firm way, adoptive parents need to tell those who make such comments that adoptive families feel uncomfortable with such terms and that as parents they are not disappointed in the least by the family they now have. They are pleased with their children, however they may have come into their family. They feel as if they, the parents, are the lucky ones to have such delightful children.

On rare occasions, adoptive families may come into contact with a crass individual who will deliberately make derogatory remarks about adoption or a specific child or parent. It is best not to argue with such a person, for it will only further upset the parent and family involved. Parents should explain the unfortunate incident to their children just as they would if they encountered someone who engaged in other bizarre or insulting behavior in public. Just as some people are physically ill and others have damaged bodies, other people are mentally or emotionally ill or have twisted minds. The comments these persons make should be totally disregarded, even though this may not be easy to do.

Many adoptive support groups and organizations work to combat the abuse and misuse of the terms that are offensive to adoptive families. They wish to portray the adoption of children as a positive concept. Like all matters involving human emotions, it can include both positive and negative aspects.

Raising children in the modern world can be a risky, unpredictable undertaking at times. But it can also be one of the most rewarding experiences of a person's life. Adoption is an alternative method of bringing children into a family who needs and wants to raise them. There are thousands of children across America and hundreds of thousands overseas whose only chance for a normal life lies in their hopes for an adoptive family. These homeless children cannot help themselves. It is up to compassionate adults to reach out to the children who wait. Many thousands of families have already traveled the road marked adoption, and whether they adopt one child or several, they know it is worth the effort. They have come to know the true beauty of adoption—the love of children.

Recommended reading

Books for Adults

Adcock, George. *Intercountry Adoption: Where Do We Go from Here?* Washington, D.C.: NACAC [North American Council on Adoptable Children], 1979. This concise handbook gives a practical overview of international adoptions and their place in the world today.

Blank, Joseph. *Nineteen Steps Up the Mountain: The Story of the Debolt Family.* Philadelphia: Lippincott, 1976. An uplifting, inspirational, yet realistic story of an incredible family that has embraced 19 children of various races and cultures as their own, many of whom are physically disabled.

Carter, Mary. *Tell Me My Name.* New York: Morrow, 1975. A captivating novel about an adopted teen who finds her biological mother and the resulting changes in the lives of all concerned, as told from the mother's point of view.

Dennis, Muriel. *Chosen Children.* Westchester, Ill.: Good News Press. A lovely inspirational look at several Christian families who have adopted special needs children, their reasons, their feelings, their stories.

Erichsen, Jean and Heino. *Gamines: How to Adopt from Latin America.* Austin, Tex.: Los Niños, 1979. A complete how-to-book on Latin-American adoption from the parents of adopted twin Colombian daughters.

Goldsein, Joseph, Anna Freud, and Albert Solnit. *Before the Best Interests of the Child.* New York: The Free Press, 1979. A comprehensive hard-hitting reference book that closely examines and weighs the criteria for government (state) intervention in the family when a child's welfare is threatened.

Jewett, Claudia. *Adopting the Older Child.* Harvard: Harvard Common Press, 1979. A comprehensive look at on the adoption of older children by one of the most respected experts in the field.

Johnson, Patricia. *Perspectives on a Grafted Tree.* Fort Wayne, Ind.: Perspectives Press, 1983. A collection of poems and artwork reflecting the many aspects of adoption as experienced by adoptive parents, adoptees, and birth parents.

Klein, Carole. *The Single Parent Experience.* New York: Walker & Company, 1973. Covers the many facets of single parenthood and features a complete chapter on single parent adoption.

Kravik, Patricia. *Adopting Children with Special Needs.* Washington, D.C.: NACAC, 1976. A beautiful close-up look at the adoption of mentally, physically, and emotionally challenged children, captured in superb photographs and the personal narratives of parents and professionals.

Krementz, Jill. *How It Feels to Be Adopted.* New York: Alfred A. Knopf, 1982. Revealing interviews with young people, ages 8 to 16, on how adoption has affected their young lives and that of their families.

Ladner, Joyce. A. *Mixed Families: Adopting Across Racial Boundaries.* Garden City, N.Y.: Doubleday, 1978. Offers a direct approach to the controversial issue of transracial adoption, including interviews with several adults raised by parents of another race.

Margolies, Marjorie. *They Came to Stay.* New York: Coward, McCann, & Georghegan, 1976. The first-person account of a single mother's struggles to adopt two lovely Asian daughters.

Marindin, Hope. *Handbook for Single Adoptive Parents.* Washington, D.C.: Committee for Single Adoptive Parents, 1981. A practical handbook of invaluable information for singles adopting American and foreign children.

McNamara, Joan and Bernard. *The Special Child Handbook.* New York: Hawthorn Books, Inc., 1977. A valuable resource for families who need guidance to help their child with special needs, that takes the family from diagnosis to a look at adulthood, and offers extensive listings of support organizations and agencies.

NACAC, Washington, D.C. This national adoption advocacy group publishes a number of current, highly respected adoption books, pamphlets, and other printed resource materials.

Menning, Barbara. *Infertility: A Guide for the Childless Couple.* Washington, D.C.: NACAC. Written by the founder of RESOLVE, the national support organization for infertile couples, this book offers a realistic view of infertility and its complexities, both physical and emotional.

OURS, Inc., Minneapolis, Minn. This large foreign adoptive family support group offers a wide variety of books and publications for adoptive, intercultural, and multi-racial families.

Plumez, Jacqueline. *Successful Adoption.* New York: Crown, 1982. A professionally written how-to guide for American and international adoption.

Sandness, Grace. *Brimming Over.* Minneapolis: Mini-World Publications, 1978. The poignant story of Grace Sandness, a handicapped adoptive mother and wife, and her remarkable multi-cultural, interracial family.

Sorosky, Arthur D. *The Adoption Triangle: The Effects of the Sealed Record on Adoptees, Birth Parents, and Adoptive Parents.* Garden City, N.Y.: Doubleday, 1979. A professional, compassionate review of the adoption policies of sealed records that have become ironclad laws in many areas.

Thompson, Jean. *The House of Tomorrow.* New York: Harper & Row, 1967. A story of adoption from a side that is rarely told: a young woman's journal as she lives in a home for unwed mothers and makes her decision to relinquish her child for adoption.

Wicker, Holly van Gulden, and Judy Walker Haavig, R.N. *Today's Child: The Health Care of IMH Infants.* Minneapolis: Today's Child Publications, 1982. While originally written for families adopting children through International Mission of Hope [India], this is an excellent resource for any family/ professional who works with children suffering from malnourishment and other deprivational problems, including parasites, skin conditions, and respiratory infections.

Books for Children and Teens

Blue, Rose. *A Quiet Place.* New York: Watts-Franklin, 1969. The story of a child's experiences in foster care.

Bunin, Catherine and Sherry. *Is That Your Sister?* New York: Pantheon, 1976. Describes the day in court as well as life in general in an interracial family.

Cohen, Robert and Ken Heyman. *The Color of Man.* New York: Random House, 1968. An account of the different races and colors of the world's peoples, including an explanation of skin tones, how and why they vary; excellent for all ages.

Lifton, Betty J. *I'm Still Me.* New York: Alfred A. Knopf, 1981. This novel for teens is an interesting, somewhat romantic story of a 16-year-old's search for her biological mother.

Lindsay, Jeanne. *Pregnant Too Soon: Adoption Is an Option.* St. Paul, Minn.: EMC Publishing, 1980. First-person narratives, comments, and advice as told by many pregnant young girls, ages 13-19. Originally compiled to help pregnant teens seriously consider adoption, as well as the two more common alternatives, abortion and raising the child as a teenage parent. Excellent reading for all teenage girls growing up in a society in which teenage sex, pregnancy, and parenthood have become a part of adolescence in general.

Livingston, Carole. *Why Was I Adopted?* Secaucus, N.J.: Lyle Stuart, Inc., 1978. A colorfully illustrated delightful explanation of adoption for those under age 10.

Milgram, Mary. *Brothers Are All the Same.* New York: Dutton, 1978. A charming narrative by the oldest daughter accompanies many excellent black-and-white photographs in this children's story of a family that has both biological and adopted children.

OURS, Inc. Minneapolis, Minn. This large foreign adoptive family support group offers a wide variety of books and publications for children and families from many different countries and cultures.

Pursell, Margaret. *A Look at Adoption*. Minneapolis, Minn.: Lerner Publications, 1978. One in a series of children's awareness books, this explanation of adoption in all its phases for children features black-and-white photographs and a foreword by Marjorie Margolies, a single adoptive parent and a television journalist.

Read, Elfreida, *Brothers by Choice*. New York: Farrar, Strauss, & Giroux, 1974. A novel about two teenage brothers, one adopted and one born into the same family, and how together they come through a personal crisis.

Roth, Arthur. *The Secret Lover of Elmtree*. New York: Fawcett, 1976. A humorous first-person novel of an adopted high school senior and the complications that develop in his life when his biological father finds him.

Simon, Norma. *Why Am I Different?* Niles, Ill.: A. Whitman, 1976. A delightful look at children as individuals, including national and religious differences.

—————————. *All Kinds of Families*. Niles, Ill.: A. Whitman, 1976. A look at families from around the world, including families formed by adoption.

Stein, Sara B. *The Adopted One*. New York: Walker & Company, 1979. A unique dual storybook for adoptive families with a large-print story for children and detailed explanations for adults about the significance of individual events and comments, all accompanied by clear black-and-white photographs, about the first time a child cries, "You're not my real parents!"

Terris, Susan. *Whirling Rainbows*. Garden City, N.J.: Doubleday, 1974. A novel of a teenage girl who spends a memorable summer at camp, looking for a link to her birth mother's American Indian heritage.

Waybill, Marjorie. *Chinese Eyes*. Scottdale, Pa.: Herald Press, 1974. A lovely story, with beautiful color illustrations, of an adopted Korean child and her mother and how they cope with a name-calling incident.

Laura L. Valenti, born and raised in St. Louis County, lives in rural southwest Missouri on the grounds of a trout hatchery, where her husband, Warren, is the assistant manager. Throughout her childhood, Ms. Valenti traveled and studied in Mexico. Both of her children, Francesca (age 8) and Ricardo (age 6), were born in El Salvador, where she and her husband served in the United States Peace Corps for over three years.

The plight of abandoned children in Central America first moved the Valentis to seriously investigate adoption, both overseas and in the United States. Two years after returning to Missouri, Ms. Valenti traveled to El Salvador alone to bring home 10-month-old Ricardo. The following year, she cofounded an adoptive parent support group in rural Missouri. "We were told it was impossible to keep such an organization going in a rural area. But then some said an American woman couldn't be an effective Peace Corps volunteer in rural Central America either; and that we'd never get our son out of El Salvador once he was adopted. I've never been good at accepting the word 'impossible.' More important, however, we've proved that people all over the country—

from the cities, the rural areas, and everywhere in between—are interested in adoption and children in need."

Ms. Valenti is knowledgeable on both American and foreign adoption and how prospective parents can best prepare themselves for the joys and the frustrations involved. She was a member of the original Governor's Adoption Task Force founded in 1983 and is now a member of Missouri's State Advisory Committee on Adoption. She is also a member of NACAC and president of an OURS chapter, in addition to being editor of *Ozark Echoes,* her state's largest regularly published adoption newsletter.

Ms. Valenti is a member of the Christian Church, Disciples of Christ. She is the youth coordinator in her local congregation, as well as a junior high Sunday school teacher and an active member of her congregation's choir.

As the president of an adoptive parent support organization, Ms. Valenti has spent the past several years answering questions of prospective and adoptive parents in person. She has now compiled that information into this, her first book.